GOD IN THE CORNERS

PERSONAL ENCOUNTERS
Discovering
God's
Fingerprints
in Remote
Corners of
our World

by Chuck Bennett

Published by
PARTNERS INTERNATIONAL
San Jose, California

Lovingly dedicated

to Jane,
who has walked the corners of the world with me
for over half a lifetime.

CONTENTS

If I ride the wings of the morning,

if I dwell by the farthest oceans,

even there your hand will guide me,

and your strength will support me.

Psalm 139:9-10

*　　*　　*　　*　　*

DEATH IN THE AFTERNOON

"**L**A-LA-LA-LA-LA-LA-LA-LA-LA-LA-LA!" Two hundred warriors screamed their blood-chilling, high-pitched uvular war cry as they charged straight across the wide clearing toward us.

Closer and closer they came, leaping and screeching and waving their spears and clubs as they ran. No point in trying to escape, so we steeled ourselves for their spears.

"So this is what it's like to die," I thought, as I wondered how my family would hear about my death.

Still closer they came. Suddenly—only a few yards away—they stopped. We held our breath. Then they turned toward a crude little reviewing stand we hadn't even had time to notice and bowed to the provincial governor who sat there. We had been certain our lives were over but, in reality, we had merely blundered—with perfect timing—into a victory celebration.

We were in the village of Bitkin in the country of Chad, on the edge of the Sahara desert. Mohamar Khadaffi's Libyan troops then occupied half of Chad, one of the poorest countries on earth. The ragtag army of Chad had just captured a major Libyan airbase inside their own country. That is what the crowd was celebrating.

But this was only the first of three life or death situations I experienced that same afternoon. The first turned out to be only a perceived danger, but the other two truly involved life and death.

After the celebration, the governor served us tea with rancid milk on the patio in front of the local government house. While we chatted, village elders in Arab robes stood around whispering together, then went inside. Suddenly, the most terrifying looking bunch of soldiers I'd ever seen drove up, straight out of the desert. I'd heard that Chadian troops shoot people who take their pictures, so I frantically hid my camera under my feet. The leader of the soldiers—a general with a scarf around his head—shook our hands, then also went inside.

The governor excused himself two or three times to join the men in the house. Each time he returned after a few minutes to chat with us again. All the while, my two companions and I sat and sipped our tea. We had no idea that just inside the house they were holding a captured rebel leader while they debated whether he should live or die. (They finally decided to make him lie flat on his face before the President of Chad while he begged for forgiveness.)

The third life or death situation that eventful afternoon was even less obvious. We had a spare seat in our small airplane, so the governor rode with us back to the capital city. As we flew, he chatted amiably with a young man who sat beside him, the trusted local assistant of a Swiss missionary. A few days later the governor ordered that same young man arrested and killed—tossed out of a helicopter high over the desert, according to local rumors.

So—all in a single afternoon—I thought I faced death from a crowd that was harmless; then I sipped tea and chatted with the governor, unaware that a man's life was hanging in the balance ten feet away; then I watched the governor in friendly conversation with a young man whom he would soon have executed.

*   *   *   *   *

First impressions certainly can be deceiving.

*   *   *   *   *

For the past 40 years I've traveled the remote corners of Planet Earth. I've lived in six countries, crisscrossed most of the world's jungles in small airplanes, and visited thousands of villages in over 85 nations. During all those journeys I've been surprised again and again to discover that my first impressions were incorrect. And again and again I have found God at work in surprising places in the corners of our world.

My parents lost their business in the great depression, so during the first ten years of my life they were dirt-poor sharecroppers in Arkansas. There they faithfully took me to a little rural Baptist church where sincere people preached a hellfire gospel that made me terrified of God's wrath.

During World War II my father trained as a machinist and found work in Michigan. There, at age 11, I made a deeply personal commitment to Christ in a church where the pastor constantly ridiculed other churches. In his view, the only true Christians were the members of our own local church and those in a few other churches pastored by his personal buddies. We had God in our tight little box and we assumed all *real* Christians would be just like us.

As I have traveled the earth since those days, I have slowly come to understand that God simply will not limit himself to the narrow boxes of my stereotypes and fears.

For 13 years I was a mission bush pilot in Latin America, then a church growth researcher in 20 countries and, for a time, director of the Presbyterian Center for Mission Studies. After that I served a dozen years as president of Mission Aviation Fellowship. Then I spent several years in Third-World relief and development as chairman of AirServ International and field director of Food for the Hungry International. Finally, since 1992, I have been president of Partners International, an agency that joint ventures with about 70 indigenous Christian ministries in 50 countries of the developing world.

Over the years, as I've walked (and flown) the remote corners of our planet, I've had opportunity to meet some of God's choicest servants, many of them people of minimal education in out-of-the-way places. The core of my faith has not changed, but my travels have taught me that God is much bigger than I had ever imagined and that my own first impressions are, often as not, mistaken. Things are frequently not what they appear to be in our complex, fascinating, sinful world.

Over and over, in ways that never cease to amaze me, I've seen God's hand in the corners of our planet. He's not lurking. He is working—always preceding, always preparing the way. And graciously inviting us to see his fingerprints everywhere.

COME TRAVEL THE CORNERS OF THAT WORLD WITH ME WHILE I TELL YOU ABOUT A FEW OF MY EXPERIENCES AND SOME OF THE THINGS GOD HAS TAUGHT ME ALONG THE WAY.

But when the Holy Spirit has come upon you, you will receive power and will tell people about me everywhere—in Jerusalem, throughout Judea, in Samaria, and to the ends of the earth.

Acts 1:8

ABANDONED IN AFGHANISTAN

"**S**urely this is still a dream!" I thought, as I woke from a nap and found myself sitting alone in a little Russian car high up in the Hindu Kush mountains of Afghanistan. "I can't be all alone in this strange place. I'll wake up soon."

I felt like Peter when the angel let him out of prison but he thought it was only a dream (Acts 12:9). Not a single person or house was anywhere in sight. To make matters worse, the sun was setting and I realized the temperature would soon be freezing cold.

Only five hours earlier I had been in a jet airliner. When we landed in Kabul, I hired an Afghan taxi driver to take me over the mountains to meet up with some missionary doctors. I spoke no Farsi and my driver's total English was the word "okay."

We followed a dirt trail over the mountains. It was so steep in places that I had to get out and stick a rock behind the rear wheel while he raced the engine and slipped the clutch to jump forward a few feet at a time. Jet lag finally won out and I dozed off as we drove. When I awoke I found myself sitting there all alone.

The keys were in the ignition and I didn't want to freeze, so after waiting about 20 minutes I decided to drive on and look for shelter. Just then the driver appeared from behind a hill about a quarter of a mile away and trotted back to join me. (I still have no idea where he had gone, nor why.) We drove on for hours, screaming down narrow dirt ledges on the sides of steep canyons. About midnight we finally arrived in the town of Bamian and woke an innkeeper who showed me to a cot with a dust-filled blanket.

The next morning I walked out on the porch of the inn and stared in amazement at two immense standing Buddhas. They are at least 150 feet tall, as high as the faces of American presidents on Mount Rushmore . . . so big that ten men can walk around on the top of each head. The images had been carved into the face of that mountain before the time of Christ.

The cliff itself was honeycombed with caves where Buddhist monks formerly lived, all connected by a network of tunnels inside the rock. Centuries after they were carved, Muslims occupied the region and chiseled away the upper faces from the huge Buddhas.

I'll admit I was feeling pretty daring and adventurous as I stood there that morning. I'd been in lots of Third-World countries before, but never any place as exotic as that.

Then God reminded me of some history I'd read that put things in perspective and made my modern adventure seem trivial by comparison. I remembered that 1,300 years before I arrived in Bamian by Russian car, Christian missionaries from Syria journeyed there *on foot* and almost certainly looked at those same gigantic Buddhas. But they didn't stop there. They kept on walking eastward another 3,000 miles, all the way to the court of China. In fact, dozens of Christian missionaries from Syria worked in China throughout the seventh and eighth centuries, while Europe was still in its Dark Age.

When we hear the word "missionary," we usually think of the Apostle Paul in the first century or else we picture European and American missionaries of the last 200 years. Somehow we overlook the *seventeen hundred years* in between. But back when my ancestors in northern Europe were still plundering and worshipping nature, Christian missionaries from the Middle East were serving in China, India, the Ukraine and elsewhere. And there have been other missionary movements over the centuries as well.

Missionaries from Europe and North America have recently become outnumbered by a dynamic new movement in countries that we used to call the "mission field." These days most mission organizations in the Western world work in close partnership with indigenous Christian missions and ministries in the developing world.

The *next era* of our 2,000-year-old missionary enterprise is already in full swing—the era of missionaries from Africa, Asia and Latin America. The founders of Partners International anticipated this change and began supporting indigenous ministries in Asia over 50 years ago.

Not long after my visit to Afghanistan, the Soviet Union invaded and occupied the country. Today civil war still rages there. It's unlikely that any American has looked on those gigantic stone Buddhas for at least 20 years. As I stood there contemplating them that morning long ago, God cut my pride down to size. He reminded me that I am not nearly as important or daring as I like to think—that far more courageous missionaries than I had already reached that far off the corner of the world and looked at those same Buddhas more than a thousand years before I did—that God always has his servants in every age to carry the Good News to their own Judeas and Samarias . . . and to the very ends of the earth.

FORGIVE ME FOR OVERESTIMATING MY IMPORTANCE, LORD. HELP ME TO KEEP YOU IN PERSPECTIVE.

*So God created people in his own image; God gathered them after
himself; male and female he created them.*
Genesis 1:27

SURPRISED BY BEAUTY

The lepers sat with vacant stares in front of their barely
standing huts while scrawny pigs rooted amid the filth and
rubbish in their yards. "This is absolutely the most depressing
place I've ever been in my life!" I thought.

As I walked through that village of primitive, pygmy-size tribal
people on the Philippine island of Palawan—most of them lepers—I felt
despondent and helpless. I could see absolutely nothing of beauty or hope
in sight. "How could we possibly help people like this?" I thought. It
almost seemed like even God had given up on them.

I should have known better. A little while later, as we were getting
ready to board our little airplane at the crude village airstrip, a tiny,
shriveled old woman came up to me and quietly handed me a gift. It was
a basket—expertly, exquisitely woven, with intricate patterns inside and
out. Its corners were trimmed with crisscrossed strips so fine it is hard to
imagine that the unfeeling fingers of a leper could have woven them.

I've kept that basket in our living room ever since. It helps remind
me that I should not judge things by first impressions. And also to remind
me that even in the most miserable of circumstances, God is still there . . .
that he has placed love and hope and appreciation of beauty within even
the most wretched of his children.

How glibly we say it, but how often we forget, that man looks on
outward appearances but God looks on the heart.

All around the world I've had the privilege of meeting many of God's
frontline heroes. Some are well-educated and experienced internationals
who fit in well in the Western world because they are outstanding com-
municators in any setting. However, many of the people on the front lines
of faith wouldn't impress you very much if you were to meet them in *our*
world. They might feel awkward and out of place in our homes and
churches, and their dress and manners would probably strike you as
unsophisticated. But back home in *their* worlds they are giants, highly
respected by their own people, and extremely effective. Like the little old

woman who gave me the basket, they have amazing talents and abilities that we might easily overlook. But God doesn't. After all, the Scriptures tell us he made them . . . and us . . . and even lepers in his own image.

With God's help, these partners in the Gospel in the far corners of our world are bringing his message of hope and love to their own people, and doing so much more effectively than we ever could.

HOW OFTEN, LORD, DO I JUDGE PEOPLE BY THEIR LOOKS OR DRESS OR SOCIAL POISE. FORGIVE ME. HELP ME TO SEE PEOPLE AS YOU DO, MADE IN YOUR IMAGE.

Instead, God deliberately chose things the world considers foolish in order to shame those who think they are wise. And he chose those who are powerless to shame those who are powerful.

I Corinthians 1:27

MY BEST TEACHERS NEVER FINISHED THE THIRD GRADE

"**P**ersonal Enemy of God." That's how the business card of the governor's secretary read down there in the steaming, stinging swamps of Tabasco, where the temperature feels as hot as Tabasco sauce. That's where God dropped me into the middle of a dynamic movement of his Spirit that blew away many of my previous assumptions.

Back in 1925, Tomás Garrido, a militant Marxist governor, took control of that roadless, swampy Mexican state and ruled it for ten years as if it were a separate country. He outlawed religion, destroyed all churches, burned all religious books, and abolished the religious names of all the towns and villages.

It was a time of total war against religion. The handful of Protestant pastors and Catholic priests then in Tabasco were all forced to flee. The governor's troops would ride their horses into Catholic churches, gather up the wooden statues of saints, burn them in the town square, roast bananas on the coals, then sweep away the ashes and hold a dance on the spot. All this, the governor said, was to "defanaticize" the people. (Graham Greene's famous novel, *The Power and the Glory,* and the subsequent Hollywood movie, were the story of a fictitious last priest in Tabasco during those tumultuous times.)

When Mexican evangelical pastors first penetrated the swamps of Tabasco a hundred years ago, most of the people there still practiced the magic and spirit appeasement of their Mayan Indian ancestors. The Catholic Church had never been strong in Tabasco. These pastors— outstanding men, well versed in theology and biblical languages— sweated and suffered and gave their lives for the people of their adopted state. After 40 years of sacrificial labor they had established only a dozen small congregations.

When the pastors were forced to flee during the time of persecution, most of the Christian believers who remained in Tabasco could not even read or write. All public worship was forbidden. Four decades of valiant work had been destroyed—or so people outside Tabasco thought. Ten years later, when the dictator was overthrown and Protestant pastors ventured there again, to their surprise they found 38 flourishing congregations of believers.

By the time I arrived in Tabasco, there were already 150 evangelical congregations. When I left nine years later, they numbered over 300. Today more than 1500 Presbyterian and Pentecostal congregations dot the Tabasco countryside. None of these was started by foreign missionaries and very few by ordained Mexican pastors. In fact, even today there are about 20 congregations for every ordained pastor in Tabasco.

I've attended lots of schools in my day. In fact, for my graduate degrees I studied under two of the world's best-known professors in their respective fields—Peter Drucker in management, and Donald McGavran in missiology. But I learned my most *valuable* lessons about life and the Christian faith from poor, barely literate farmers down there in the swamps of Southeast Mexico—people who still clear their fields with *machetes* and plant their corn and beans in holes made with pointed sticks.

That's where my *real* education took place. That's where I began to understand how God works in our world through believers of many cultures and backgrounds, including people with little formal training or sophistication. Those people showed me with their lives a kind of wisdom, commitment, maturity and effectiveness that simply cannot be taught in classrooms.

When God dropped me into the middle of that movement of his Spirit, I saw things all around me that simply didn't fit what I had been taught in theological school or in my home church. Punctuality was not high on their list of virtues, of course, since few of them had clocks. I saw overtones of the old folk-Catholicism in their worship services, and I was shocked to find they used marriage as a means of evangelism. (Very effectively, by the way.) In fact, they did many things that I had been taught were wrong. But I could not deny that the hand of God was at work in what I was seeing all around me. Nor could I deny the sincerity of the faith of the farmer-evangelists and village lay leaders with whom I worked every day.

As I came to know the people and the local dialect better and spent hundreds of nights out in the villages, I became more and more impressed by the depth of their biblical knowledge, the consistency of their faith, their deep understanding of human nature, and their overall practical wisdom.

These were people who had never finished the third grade nor traveled 50 miles from where they were born. Yet, I was surprised and humbled to find they knew the Bible and practiced their faith far better than I. That was my *real* education.

Prominent leaders and formal education have their place, of course. But unsung heroes, like those people down in the steaming swamps of Tabasco who taught me with their lives, are the ones who are quietly changing our world. Actually, through the centuries it has always been untrained, unsophisticated Christians—not prominent leaders—who have won the vast majority of new believers to Christ. And that's still the way it is today in the parts of the world where Christianity is expanding rapidly.

How easily we confuse education with wisdom, and theological jargon with spirituality. But God continues to choose things the world considers foolish to shame those of us who think we are wise.

LORD, HELP ME TO BE WILLING TO LISTEN WHEN YOU SPEAK TO ME THROUGH THE SUPPOSEDLY UNEDUCATED PEOPLE OF OUR WORLD.

*Then Jesus said, Come to me, all of you who are weary and carry
heavy burdens, and I will give you rest. Take my
yoke upon you. Let me teach you.*
Matthew 11:28, 29

"WHY CAN'T YOU DO SOMETHING?"

The Maasai woman in bright red clothing held her crusty-headed baby up to my face and pointed at the scabies.
"Why can't you do something to help us get water?" she
demanded. "If we had water we could wash our children and
they wouldn't have skin and eye diseases like this."

We stood in front of a tin shed church only a two-hour drive over a
rocky trail from the modern city of Nairobi. It took a lot of nerve for that
woman to confront me—a visiting *Mzungu* (white person)—but she and
her people were desperate. Every two days, like the other women in her
settlement, she leaves before dawn to walk eight or ten miles to the nearest
water, then eight or ten miles home, carrying four gallons (34 pounds) of
water on her back.

Imagine, only four gallons of water to meet all the needs of her
family for two days. Not enough to wash her children, or their clothes, or
her dishes. Barely enough to survive on.

This woman is a sincere Christian. Why, then, must she watch her
children suffer and sometimes die? Is it because she has less faith than I?
I sincerely doubt it. Is it because she doesn't work hard enough? That's a
joke.

Do her children suffer because she doesn't love them as much as we
do ours? The look on her face and the courage it took for her to confront
a foreigner like me proved that a lie.

The woman's face haunts me still. "I hear you," I said through the
interpreter. "I promise you I will try my best to get money to drill a well
here."

The Kenyan government claims it can't afford to drill wells in Maasai
territory. Yet, the very week I was there, in 1996, the government announced
the purchase of an Airbus jumbo jet for the exclusive use of its top officials
on their rare trips to other countries.

Ironically, only two hours after my encounter with that courageous mother I was soaking off the dust of the road in a deep tub of water in my hotel room in Nairobi. I'll admit that was one warm bath I simply couldn't enjoy.

The woman who confronted me was a Christian, but most of the Maasai are not. For thousands of years these extremely traditional people have been herding their cattle throughout present-day Kenya and Tanzania, moving from water hole to water hole. But the population has mushroomed and land is now scarce, so the Maasai have been pushed out into the semidesert wastelands where life is desperate.

Their government may show little concern for the Maasai, but a dedicated group of Kenyan Christians does care about them. *Deeply.* Led by a human dynamo named Yusuf, these volunteers from the churches of Nairobi give the only outside help to a region that contains about 30,000 Maasai. Assisted by Partners International, they preach, they teach, and they help heal the sick.

Yusuf and his team have recruited and trained several Maasai evangelists and nurses. Volunteer doctors and nurses from Nairobi also hold clinics in Maasai territory. But over half the ailments they treat are skin and eye diseases that could easily be prevented if the mothers merely had enough water to bathe their children.

The Maasai people are more willing to listen to the Gospel today than ever before. Their traditional way of life is failing them and so is their traditional religion. Already many have turned to Christ and many more are searching. Could it be because no one except the Christians seems to want to help them?

Every time I think of that Maasai woman, I want to ask God "Why?" Why do some of us have it so easy while others—even sincere Christians— have to live such lives of misery? From our perspective, something's clearly out of whack. Certainly that Maasai woman qualifies as one who is weary and carries heavy burdens. And certainly Jesus can give her spiritual rest and peace. (I think he has already.) But I still struggle over her lack of relief from the physical burdens that will surely drive her to an early grave.

LORD, SHE ASKS FOR SO LITTLE—THINGS SO BASIC I DON'T EVEN THINK ABOUT THEM. AND THERE ARE SO MANY OTHERS LIKE HER. HOW DO I JUSTIFY THEIR NEED AND MY ABUNDANCE? LORD, USE ME TO HELP GIVE THEM WATER FOR LIFE AND THE WATER OF LIFE.

*Soon a gale swept down upon them as they rowed, and the sea grew very
rough . . . . They were terrified, but he called out to them, "I am here!
Don't be afraid!" Then they were eager to let him in.*
John 6:18-20

BORNEO CASTAWAYS

"**J**ust tell this guy to turn the boat around, Ken!" I screamed
above the wind. "This is no time for protocol!"

We were two or three miles off the east coast of Borneo, heading for
the island of Tarakan where we had left our airplane. The night was pitch
black. All we could see was the phosphorescent glow of the wave crests
as they hit the front of our big canoe and sent their spray over our heads.

"How did I let us get into this mess?" I thought, mentally kicking
myself. We had no life preservers, no compass and no flashlight. The
outboard motor—our only steering device—was coughing and sputtering.
If it stopped, we knew we would turn broadside to the waves and roll
over, so we tied our documents to the boat with our shoestrings. If we
drowned, at least someone would eventually find the boat and notify our
families.

"Tell him to head for shore, Ken," I said to my companion who
spoke Indonesian. "He's the captain," Ken replied. "We have to trust
him." But I'd had enough! That's when I yelled to Ken that he should
forget about protocol.

Jesus didn't come walking on the water that night, but he did hear our
prayers. It seemed like an eternity before we finally saw the faint outline
of the treetops on the shore. A few minutes later we slipped among the
trees into a mangrove tidal swamp. The next few hours seemed like
another eternity as we clung to tree branches to keep from being swept
back into the swamp by the tide. What a night! Mud, mosquitoes, wet
clothes, cold wind, Ken and I wedged side by side in the bottom of the
canoe. But we were alive!

The bravest person by far that pitch-black night was our barefoot
boatman who, after the tide reversed, jumped out again and again into the
unseen muck to free our boat so we wouldn't be left stranded in the mud.

Ah, but the dawn at the end of that night of hell was the most unfor-
gettable of all as it broke on a sea so smooth it was hard to believe it was
liquid. The dawn of the previous day had been equally wonderful, like a

foretaste of heaven, complete with angel choir. At least I thought I must be hearing angels as I slowly awoke to the sound of an incredibly beautiful choir singing softly outside the window of our hut in the Kerayan valley, deep in the heart of Borneo.

Missionaries reached the Kerayan people back in the 1930s by traveling up the wild rivers for a solid month. (It took us an hour in our small airplane.) At great sacrifice the missionaries eventually won a few of the local people to Christ. Then came the War. Japanese troops invaded the Kerayan valley and slaughtered the missionaries in cold blood.

World War II was followed by the struggle for Indonesian independence from the Dutch; then by a local war between Indonesia and Malaysia. So nearly 20 years passed before missionaries were again allowed back into the Kerayan valley. When they arrived, they discovered to their great surprise that virtually all the 10,000 people there were already Christians.

By the time I visited the Kerayan in 1973, every village had a church and trained pastor. Their amazing choirs could sing dozens of hymns in full harmony from memory, as beautifully as most church choirs in Europe or America. And they had three Bible institutes.

Since they already had all the pastors they needed, I asked them why they had three theological schools to train more. "We are training missionaries," they replied. And they were. In fact, the Kerayan church was already sending its missionaries to many other tribes of former headhunters throughout the huge jungle-covered island of Borneo.

Each missionary candidate was taught a trade, such as carpentry. When he and his family were sent out, their churches gave them enough money to cover their expenses for three months. After that they were on their own to win the trust of the people, learn the local language and customs, and give them the Gospel. All the while they supported themselves by practicing their trades.

The jungle-covered limestone ridges and sinkholes of East Borneo are so incredibly hostile to travel that it can take up to two months to journey by land and sea to another tribe that may be only a hundred miles away. Direct overland travel is virtually impossible. The Kerayan missionaries would follow one river system out to the coast, wait for a coastal boat to take them to the mouth of another river, then spend weeks slowly poling their way upstream to their destination. Men could survive such trips, but it was too much for families with children. In a small airplane the same trip takes about 45 minutes. But airplanes cost money and the Kerayan churches didn't want handouts from the missions, so they found a creative solution.

The Kerayan people in their isolated valley needed cloth, salt, lanterns, and other trade goods from the coast. The coastal people, on the other hand, craved vegetables that would only grow in the cool interior. So the Kerayan churches hired small airplanes to fly trade goods into their valley and carry their fresh vegetables to the coast on the return flights, where they were sold to pay for the flights. While the planes were in the interior they made side trips to carry missionary families out to their posts among other interior tribes.

Indigenous missionary movements like this one are springing up all around the world today. Some of them need no outside financial help at all. Many others *do* need our help. But they don't want welfare. They want partners who will respect their dignity and creativity and treat them as equals. And that's the way it should be.

LORD, COULD YOU GIVE ME JUST A SMALL MEASURE OF THE ZEAL OF THE KERAYAN MISSIONARIES, AND THOUSANDS OF OTHERS LIKE THEM ALL AROUND THE WORLD?

Lord why do you stand so far away? Proud and wicked people viciously oppress the poor . . . . The helpless are overwhelmed and collapse; they fall beneath the strength of the wicked. Lord, you know the hopes of the helpless. Surely you will listen to their cries and comfort them.
You will bring justice to the orphans and the oppressed,
so people can no longer terrify them.
Psalms 10:1, 2, 10, 17 & 18

HOLOCAUST FROM MY WINDOW

M *onrovia, Liberia. May 1994.* I gaze from my hotel window at children playing happily in a churchyard across the street, a scene of total peace and tranquility. Yet I know that in that very same church not long before, 600 women and children screamed and begged for mercy as soldiers sprayed bullets into their huddled bodies, while the president of the country looked on.

The mass slaughter in Liberia in recent years has been matched only by the killing fields of Cambodia and the genocide of Rawanda. To picture the sheer scope of this horror, let's compare Liberia to the United States. Imagine, if you can, what if every man, woman and child in California had been slaughtered and everyone else west of the Mississippi had fled to Mexico and Canada? Then imagine all remaining Americans jammed into the larger cities, with the entire countryside virtually empty except for bands of armed teenage bandits. *That describes Liberia today!*

The slaughter has been senseless and random. Stories abound of barrels full of human heads . . . of soldiers slitting open the dead bodies of pregnant women after placing bets on the gender of the unborn children.

I meet with the acting president of Liberia in his office in the Presidential Palace. As we talk, the door pops open and an arrogant man carrying a swagger stick enters. Uninvited, he asks what we are doing, shakes our hands and sits down. The head of state is clearly displeased but says nothing. Later I learn that the arrogant man is a rebel general who personally ordered thousands to be executed.

Something has gone terribly wrong in Liberia!

May 1996. A few months ago it looked like peace had finally come. The rebel leaders agreed to a coalition government and crowds cheered as they entered the capital city. Refugees in neighboring countries were preparing to come home. International relief and development agencies poured into Liberia to assist the returnees and help rebuild the country. At last there was hope.

Then the madness started all over again. All-out warfare between the rebel armies. Bodies of teenage soldiers lie in the streets for days. Virtually every building in the city is looted. Two thousand diplomats and foreign residents are evacuated at night by U.S. Marine helicopters.

The new fighting first began around the same hotel where I had stayed. The one from which I had earlier looked out on the children playing peacefully in the churchyard. Some of the hotel rooms were destroyed by rocket-propelled grenades—perhaps even my room.

As I edit these notes from my diary, a peace of sorts has returned to Liberia and international relief agencies are again trying to feed the starving. Yet, in the countryside, rebel soldiers are blocking relief vehicles while hundreds of children and old people die of starvation every day.

If you doubt the doctrine of original sin and human depravity, you have only to visit Liberia. As someone has said, "If you think there's good in everybody, then you haven't met everybody."

Yet, in the midst of all that horror, there were countless signs of hope and bravery. I saw people who had lost every earthly possession planning optimistically for the future. I visited a school of 1200 students meeting in a shell of a building. Its well-trained Christian teachers were working for less than four U.S. dollars per month. I saw 50 elderly people who had no surviving families being lovingly cared for in a wreck of a house by 14 young Liberian Christian volunteers, most of whom were themselves unemployed.

I listened to a Kpelle tribal clan chief who had come through rebel lines to tell us that 4,000 of his people were ready to become Christians because of the life and witness of one of our rural workers while he and his family had themselves been prisoners of the rebels. For nearly four years, they lived mostly on wild yams. They lost a child to measles and suffered beatings and torture. The wife escaped rape by a rebel soldier only because another soldier shot the attacker. Yet, through it all, they lovingly helped their neighbors.

The evil in places like Liberia is beyond my comprehension. I simply can't understand how some people can enjoy torturing and killing, while others can be triumphant in God's grace as they face death. But then, the Psalmist didn't understand it either.

I do know that God hasn't abandoned Liberia after all. In the midst of their agony he hears their cries, comforts them, and gives them unbelievable courage.

LORD, IF I AM EVER PUT TO THE TEST LIKE MY BROTHERS AND SISTERS IN LIBERIA, I PRAY YOU WILL GIVE ME THEIR KIND OF COURAGE; NOT ONLY TO SURVIVE, BUT TO BECOME A WOUNDED HEALER.

*If I ride the wings of the morning, if I dwell by the farthest oceans,
even there your hand will guide me, and your strength
will support me.*
Psalms 139:9-10

CONQUERING JUNGLE BARRIERS

It's *March 1955.* A tiny mission floatplane lands on a small lake high in the mountains of Dutch New Guinea. This is the first contact between outsiders and half a million stone-age people who didn't even know the outside world existed.

A week later—*my very first day as a young missionary recruit*—I am handed a roll of film to develop . . . pictures of that historic faraway airplane landing. And just a few months after that world headlines screamed the story of Jim Elliott, Nate Saint, and three other intrepid missionaries in Ecuador, killed by savage "Aucas" while trying to penetrate that Amazon jungle frontier.

So my own career in missions began precisely when the last great jungle and mountain barriers that isolated many primitive peoples from the Gospel were finally being breached.

Later, as a mission pilot, I crisscrossed the vast jungle of southern Venezuela, flying beside the world's highest waterfalls and threading my way between jungle-capped, mile-high stone pinnacles called *tepúes* that rise straight out of the vast Amazon rainforest like islands in the sky. We were looking for the distinctive circular villages of the primitive, elusive Yanomami people. And we found them, long before they were featured in National Geographic.

In Borneo I dropped gifts to former headhunters who were hacking out the first airstrips in the heart of that Texas-size, jungle-covered island. Back then our goal was to conquer earth's jungle and mountain barriers in order to locate and reach all the isolated tribes of the world with the message of Christ's love.

And with God's help we succeeded.

The jungles haven't all disappeared yet, of course, although they *are* being destroyed all too rapidly. But virtually all the former lost, hidden and untouched tribes on earth have now been contacted with the Gospel. The "jungle hero" phase of missions that Christians of my generation grew up hearing about is over. Now a completely new way of spreading the Good News is already in full swing.

Not long ago I stood before a little Christian church building near Jogjakarta, Indonesia, in the heartland of the proud Javanese people whose complex civilization dates back thousands of years. To my amazement I was told that the church I was looking at had been started by a student at a nearby seminary who had come from the heart of Irian Jaya, former Dutch New Guinea. He was the son of one of the unclothed, stone-age tribesmen who first become aware of the outside world when a little airplane dropped missionaries into their midst—the airplane in the pictures I developed on my first day as a missionary candidate.

This dark-skinned son of a stone-age tribesman had not only completed seminary, he had also been able to gain the trust of the proud, sophisticated Javanese—a completely different race—winning many of them to Christ and planting a church among them.

Nor is this man's story unique. Children of Dyak headhunters—the so-called "wild men of Borneo"—have now gone out as missionaries all over their own huge island and even to Java and Sumatra. In South America, "Auca" and Yanomami Christians are now carrying the Good News to their fellow tribesmen in the Amazon jungle. Today missionaries from Nigeria serve in the slums of Chicago, while Native American missionaries work in Siberia and Mongolia. Our old stereotypes of white missionaries in pith helmets are simply out of date. We have truly entered a new era in missions.

God gave my generation airplanes and radios that enabled us to fly on "the wings of the morning . . . to the farthest oceans" in order to conquer the jungle and mountain barriers that held back the spread of the Gospel. Today he is using indigenous missionaries to conquer even more formidable barriers in human hearts.

Christians in the Western world were just beginning to work in partnership with indigenous, non-Western missionaries back when my flying colleagues and I were conquering jungle barriers. Today opportunities for this kind of international partnership abound.

The population of the world has approximately doubled during my adult lifetime, but the number of Christians in the non-Western world has at least quadrupled. And the number of Third-World Christians who today serve as missionaries is probably *20 or 30 times as great.* For them, the barriers of culture, language and nationality are usually far less than for us.

Today the growth of Christ's Church in the non-Western world exceeds anything we even dreamed of a generation ago. In fact, we are now living in the time of the greatest numerical expansion of the Christian faith in history. Isn't it great that God allows you and me to have a part in this fantastic movement?

LORD, HELP ME TO KNOW HOW I CAN BEST HELP YOUR FRONTLINE SERVANTS IN TODAY'S WORLD, SO DIFFERENT FROM THE WORLD OF MY YOUTH.

*Then Peter replies, "I see very clearly that God doesn't show partiality.
In every nation he accepts those who fear him and do what is right."*
Acts 10:34-35

THROUGH THE EYE OF A FLY

I slammed my airplane onto the tiny airstrip beside the
church at Santo Domingo just seconds before the full force
of the storm hit. I was happy to find a place—any place—
where I could make an emergency landing. It was the strongest
storm in my 13 years in that area.

Only one family lived near the airstrip in that roadless area of
swamps and scattered corn patches. With typical Mexican hospitality,
the family took me in and gave me the best they had—a hammock in
their two-room hut and a bedsheet to keep me warm. The storm
roared on, so they were stuck with me for the next three days.

Hosting a *gringo* pilot was a new experience for that family. Their
world was limited to their island in the swamps. They had no radio.
Only the husband had ever traveled to the nearest city, a mere 20
miles away. So I was a real novelty and the husband and children
plied me with questions all the first day, while the wife worked in her
dirt-floor cookshed, a few feet from the house.

By the second day they had become used to my presence, and by
the third day—while the storm still raged—the family returned to
their normal routines and I was almost unnoticed, like a fly on the
wall. That's when I began to see things that changed my whole
perception of their culture.

You need to understand that I had already lived in that area for
several years. I spoke the local dialect of Spanish and I'd slept out in
the villages hundreds of nights. I was perfectly relaxed there and I
thought I knew the culture well. But always before I had been an
invited guest, usually as part of a teaching or preaching team, so I had
only seen people on their best behavior.

This time I was alone and uninvited. This time it wasn't for a
special event. And this time I stayed around long enough to see their
normal family life.

I was uncomfortable—but not surprised—each time the woman

served food to her husband and me at the table in their house, while she and the children ate standing up around the central firepit in their separate cookshed. After all, women always served men in that culture where the man is king. There the woman's role is to care for the children, wash clothes by hand, and *always, always* have food ready whenever it strikes the man's fancy to come home. Men like my host, who had become evangelical Christians, no longer beat their wives or came home drunk, but they were still cock of the roost in their home. I knew the culture well—or so I thought.

On the third day, while the kids were out in the cookshed, I overheard the husband and wife in quiet conversation about one of the children who was having problems. That's when I saw (and heard) something I had never before observed in that culture—two mature, loving Christian parents struggling together *as equals* to decide what was best for their child, earnestly searching for God's leading about what they should do.

Suddenly I realized that I had been judging a people I thought I knew well by external symbols alone—things like where the wife ate and how she served her husband. Without thinking, I had assumed that if a wife couldn't even eat with her husband, she certainly had no voice in family decisions. In other words, I had been judging them by the standards of *my* culture, not theirs.

It's inevitable, I suppose, that we measure other peoples and other cultures by the standards of our own. That's all most of us have to go on. Anthropologists call it "ethnocentrism." It's been the indirect cause of most wars and prejudice and oppression down through the ages—part of our self-centered need to feel that we are better than others.

The early apostles struggled constantly over whether one must first keep Jewish laws in order to become a Christian. Peter needed a vision about eating unclean animals before he could believe that God would accept Cornelius. Paul battled with the "judaizers" throughout his ministry.

I'll admit I'm still not comfortable with the way women and servants are often treated in other cultures—not to mention in our own. But when I find myself in situations like that, I try to remember the time I was a fly on the wall in the house near the airstrip in Santo Domingo. I try to remind myself that my perceptions may be incomplete . . . that God has created an incredible symphony of cultures in his world, each with its own limitations, but each also with its own beauty . . . that there are always hidden layers of both good and evil in every culture.

HELP ME, LORD, NOT TO JUMP TO CONCLUSIONS ABOUT OTHER PEOPLE'S MOTIVES JUST BECAUSE THEIR CUSTOMS AREN'T MINE.

A giant Buddha of Bamian in Afghanistan, showing caves where monks lived.
(Page 5)

The woman in Bangladesh whose life was changed by $90 in loans.
(Page 27)

A giant elephant of Marsabit, afraid of a row of fence posts. (Page 35)

Greeting Muslim elders in a village in Tanzania. (Page 40)

So if we have enough food and clothing, let us be content.
I Timothy 6:8
Peter said, "I don't have any money for you. But I'll give you what I
have. In the name of Jesus Christ of Nazareth, get up and walk!"
Acts 3:6

NINETY DOLLARS TO BUY HAPPINESS

The woman's face fairly glowed as she stood before her two-room mud hut in a small village in Bangladesh. I'll never forget it.

"Before we received the loans," she told me, "we ate only once a day. My children were naked and my *sari* was made of used cloth. But now," her eyes flashed with enthusiasm, "we eat *twice* a day! My children have clothes, I buy new cloth for my *sari,* and we have a metal roof over our bedroom." She spread her arms as if to encompass her entire house and family. "Now," she exclaimed, "I am happy!"

A $30 loan that made it possible for this woman to set up a tiny business. She paid it back in ten months, then received another loan for $60. After that was paid off, she was on her own. That was all it took for her to break out of a cycle of destitution. Those two tiny loans—and her hard work and sweat—transformed her life and that of her family. She needed so very little to make her happy.

We completed *4,000* such loans in Bangladesh—most of them to women—while I worked with a Christian development agency. Not one of those loans was backed by collateral, but every single one was paid back in full. And all but two were paid on time. Any loan officer in an American bank would be green with envy over such a record.

It's impossible—when you work among the poorest of the poor—to minister effectively to their spiritual needs and ignore their physical and social needs. Besides, poor and needy people usually respond more readily to the Christian message than affluent people.

The poor are already well aware of their personal needs and their own vulnerability; and that's the first step in admitting their need for God. That's why our overseas partners who follow the example of Jesus and minister to *both* the spiritual and physical needs of their people, are also able to start thousands of new churches.

When we meet an obviously poor person, how easy it is to assume that he or she must be irresponsible or lazy, and probably looking for handouts. When I catch myself thinking that way, I jerk myself back to reality by remembering that woman in Bangladesh, standing before her mud-walled house with her arms outstretched in happiness.

Peter had no silver or gold to give, but he gave healing to the lame man. We gave only a tiny amount of money to the woman in Bangladesh, and even that only as a loan. That's all she needed to be able to stand on her own feet, provide for her family, and find a measure of contentment and personal worth.

When God brings desperately needy people across my path—whether at home or overseas—it's so easy to find excuses to pass them by. I do it all the time. Yet often they need so very little to regain their dignity.

LORD, YOU'VE GIVEN ME SO MUCH, YET I STILL COMPLAIN. HELP ME —TODAY—TO BE CONTENT WITH WHATEVER YOU GIVE ME. AND MAKE ME MORE WILLING TO HELP OTHERS.

But then some of the men who had been Pharisees before their conversion stood up and declared that all Gentile converts must be circumcised and be required to follow the law of Moses.

Acts 15:5

OF MULES AND MISSION

I turned in my saddle to say something to the man riding the horse behind me. When I turned back, the man and horse in front of me had vanished! Gone! Poof! In a couple of seconds. I couldn't believe my eyes.

We were walking our horses slowly and gingerly along a foot-wide ledge across a steep, bare mountainside in the coffee country of northwest Colombia. Our local Colombian guide trotted impatiently up ahead on his mule, shouting for us to move faster. But we were too terrified by the narrow trail and steep dropoff.

While I was still in shock at the missing horse and rider, I heard a shout and looked down. There below us the horse was on its back, legs flailing, stopped by the only clump of bushes on the entire mountainside. The rider had jumped clear and clung to the bushes to keep from sliding into the raging river below. His horse had literally fallen off a path where mules trot easily, even at night.

Mules are amazing animals. Mountain people love them because they are surefooted. They're also stronger than most horses, less susceptible to disease, less finicky about food, and they can get up to running speed faster than horses. With these advantages, why didn't mules replace horses long ago?

Unfortunately, mules have a major drawback. A mule is a hybrid, the offspring of a mare and a jackass—two different species—*and hybrids are sterile.* They cannot reproduce themselves.

Sometimes our attempts to evangelize people of other cultures remind me of mules. With the best of intentions we often try to make copies of our American Christianity. We assume that all really good Christians should have nice buildings, clearly defined goals and, of course, be neat and punctual . . . just like us. (Like Professor Higgins' lament in *My Fair Lady,* "Why can't a woman be like *me*?")

Perhaps we subconsciously assume that since God has blessed us with so many material blessings, we must somehow be more spiritual. So we want others to be like us. We fail to recognize that when we try to produce carbon copies of our American churches overseas they are, in fact, hybrids. They may look good at first but, like mules, they will be unable to reproduce themselves with their own resources.

There's nothing new about our desire to have our converts look and act just like us. Many of the early Jewish Christians sincerely believed that converts among the Gentiles must adopt all the customs and laws of the Jews.

The homegrown variety of Christianity in other cultures may look less impressive to us at first, but it keeps on growing year after year, long after foreign money and foreign leadership have been removed, because it is rooted in the local culture. Over the long haul the results will be many times greater.

By contrast, "hybrid Christianity"—Christ presented in the trappings of American or European or even Korean culture—can actually inoculate a population against the Gospel. "If we must act like foreigners in order to become Christians," the local people may think, "then we want no part of it!" Wouldn't you or I feel the same?

Most of our American evangelical Christianity is "home grown" and deeply rooted in our own culture. After their war of independence from England, most Americans rejected the Anglican Church of the hated English. Baptists in America were few and Methodists had only recently arrived. Presbyterians were in the best position to become the dominant religion. But Presbyterians insisted that all their pastors be trained in formal theological schools.

As settlers moved west into the vast frontier territories, the Presbyterians simply couldn't train enough new clergy to meet the demand. Furthermore, most of the ministers trained in theology and biblical languages in seminaries back East didn't want to move to the rough-and-tumble settlements in the West. Many of those who did go west were—pardon the analogy—often like hybrid mules, superior in some ways but unable to reproduce themselves in that environment.

By contrast, the unsophisticated frontier Baptist and Methodist churches were led by farmer preachers and circuit riders who were trained on the job. They learned by doing, often mentored by more experienced pastors. They were rooted in the local culture and completely self-sustaining, able to reproduce themselves indefinitely. As a result, they started 10 or 20 times as many new churches on the frontier as the

Presbyterians. Today Baptists and Methodists are in many ways still the dominant indigenous religion of the American heartland, whereas there are now probably more Muslims than Presbyterians in the United States. (Incidentally, I currently worship at a Presbyterian church.)

Mules are great for many things. So are our American churches in their own environment. But if we insist that Christians in other countries and cultures should act and think just like us, our efforts may turn out to be as sterile as mules.

FORGIVE ME, FATHER, FOR CONFUSING MY OWN CULTURE WITH THE ESSENCE OF MY FAITH—FOR MY PRIDE IN THINKING, "WHY CAN'T CHRISTIANS EVERYWHERE BE LIKE ME?"

Then Jesus said to his critics, "I have a question for you.
Is it legal to do good deeds on the Sabbath?"
Luke 6:9

CONFESSIONS OF A BODY SMUGGLER

"**H**ermano, my daughter is dead," the man sobbed. The beautiful ten-year-old Tzeltal Indian girl in the back seat of my airplane was desperately ill, but bad weather blocked my way over the mountains to the hospital. After turning back several times, I tried a different direction and finally managed to land on a grass airstrip near the town of Comitan. While I rushed to find a car that would take us to a doctor, I left the girl and her father in the plane. I soon located a taxi and returned to get the girl, only to discover her crying father cradling her dead body.

The father spoke little Spanish and had even less money. How would he arrange to bury his daughter in a strange Mexican town where neither he nor I knew anyone? Moreover, being buried far from home is the worst tragedy imaginable for an Indian. How would the spirit of the girl find its way back home?

But Mexican laws are very precise. The dead must be buried within 24 hours. Furthermore, no body may be transported without a special order from a judge, and a special order could take days. It was a catch-22. Next to impossible.

I just couldn't leave the man there at the airstrip with his daughter's body. What should I do? By now the taxi driver, the soldier who guarded the airstrip, and three mechanics working there on a plane all knew about the girl. I walked up to each one of them individually, looked him straight in the eye and said, "The girl has died. I'm going to take her back home. And you are not going to report me, are you?" One by one they nodded in agreement.

Then I climbed into my plane, took off and threaded my way back through the bad weather to the jungle village I had brought them from. We arrived at dusk, so I had to spend the night there shivering in a hammock.

During my years in that area we flew scores of critically ill Indians out of the jungle to government hospitals. They were accustomed to small airplanes and had no fear of flying, but most of them had never seen a car. Some of them totally panicked when we landed in the city and asked them to get into one of those growling monsters with big round eyes.

Inevitably, some of these critically ill people died. We had carried them away from home, so naturally their families expected us to take their bodies back. That's why I found myself smuggling dead bodies.

Normally I'm a stickler for the law. I even obey speed limits. But what do you do when laws are made by a dominant culture that neither understands nor cares about the values of the radically different cultures under its control?

How could I tell the Indians I was there to share Christ's love with them, then refuse to help them in their time of greatest need and crisis? That's why I was willing to risk losing my license—and even jail or expulsion—in order to help them. Fortunately, sympathetic Mexican doctors often covered for us.

As long as I live I'll remember the sobbing cry of the brother of a badly injured Indian I had flown out of the jungle. As we listened to the injured man's death rattle, the brother cradled his head in his lap and cried over and over, "*¡Mi hermano está muerto!* My brother is dead! My brother is dead!" We hid the body overnight and I flew it home at the crack of dawn. What else could I do?

The Mexican laws were perfectly reasonable from their point of view. They had no embalming facilities, so they buried quickly. They prohibited transport without a court order to minimize foul play. But Mexican authorities cared little about the incredible horror the Indians—even Christian Indians—felt at the prospect of being buried away from home.

Once two men showed up at our door in the middle of the night carrying the body of their mother, wrapped in a grass mat. She had died that day in the government hospital and a doctor had kindly looked the other way while they removed her body. They wanted us to fly them home to their mountain village. They had no way of knowing that we had already promised to fly the governor of the state and his party to *the very same airstrip* early the next day for a visit to a mission clinic just over the hill.

What should we do? Dead bodies don't keep.

First thing the next morning, my two associates flew in the governor and his aides while I waited by the radio for their signal that the visitors had walked from the airstrip over the hill to the clinic. Then, carrying the brothers and their mother's body, I approached the airstrip very low from the opposite direction, landed short and kept the engine running while one son flipped his mother's body over his shoulder and they disappeared into the nearby tall corn. Then I took off as quietly as I could, with reduced power, and flew away just above the treetops.

I know this sounds crude. Even shocking. But how can I describe for you the tender love and respect the two men showed for their mother, or the incredible gratitude in their faces as they quickly thanked me before ducking into the cornfield with their mother's body.

LORD, WHY DO MOST OF MY CHOICES SEEM TO BE BETWEEN THINGS THAT ARE NEITHER BLACK NOR WHITE? HELP ME, FATHER, TO BE WILLING TO TAKE RISKS IN THE GREY AREAS OF LIFE.

Many people, including some of the Jewish leaders, believed in him. But
they wouldn't admit it to anyone because of their fear.
John 12:42

THE FEARFUL GIANTS OF
MARSABIT MOUNTAIN

When I first saw them, far across a field, they looked like buildings walking.

The great elephants of Marsabit Mountain are probably the largest land animals alive on earth today. For thousands of years these elephants have been lords of a unique patch of tropical forest within the vast desert of northern Kenya. There, cut off from contact with other elephants, they have developed into their present gigantic size.

In the early 1980s drought destroyed all the cattle of the nomadic Samburu and Rendili tribes who lived in the desert around the mountain. Their sole means of livelihood was gone, so the government assigned them fertile lands to farm on the edge of the Marsabit Mountain game preserve.

But nobody asked permission from the elephants. They ripped up the gardens of the settlers and tossed their huts aside like doll houses. They also chased and killed any settler who ventured too close. The situation was desperate. Then an enterprising American relief volunteer suggested electric fences.

All it took to enclose a ten-mile loop around a village and its fields was one car battery, a solar panel charger, a transformer, and two wires mounted on tall fence posts. It worked like a charm. One touch of their sensitive trunks to the stinging wires and the massive beasts stayed clear. Soon several villages had encircled their houses and crops safely behind the charged wires.

After a couple of years the batteries failed, leaving the wires un-charged. But the elephants wouldn't come near. Then wires were broken and stolen. Still the elephants stayed clear.

How preposterous and comical to see the world's largest, most powerful land animals terrified by a row of bare fence posts. When I saw the wireless elephant fence of Marsabit, I couldn't help thinking that some of my own actions are just as ridiculous as those elephants. We humans are not the largest, but we are the most intelligent creatures in God's creation. Yet we also allow our lives to be controlled by irrational fear based on painful past experiences.

Someone ridicules my faith, so I keep quiet about it in public. Or, someone snubs me, so I stay away from him and his friends. Or, I try to help someone in need, but that person takes advantage of me, so I quit trying to help others.

One painful experience and I vow, "Never again!"

As I grow older the list of my painful experiences—the times I've touched the charged wire and felt its sting—grows longer and longer. And each time I make another entry in my catalog of experiences that I plan to avoid at all costs. But in protecting myself I miss so much joy and so many of God's blessings.

I'm not alone in trying to avoid unpleasant experiences. "You shouldn't give money to people in poor countries," I hear some folks say. "They'll take advantage of you, and it makes them dependent." That can happen, of course. But we could use the same logic to say we should outlaw all marriage because some husbands abuse their wives.

When it comes right down to it, most of us are about as timid and fearful as the great elephants of Marsabit, or the first-century Jewish leaders who refused to admit they believed in Jesus.

Nowhere in the Scriptures do I find where God has promised me that I won't be let down or deceived—that my tender trunk won't get zapped from time to time. But I believe he expects me to keep trying, keep risking pain, keep looking for new openings of service in his Kingdom.

LORD, GIVE ME THE COURAGE TO TEST THE FENCES AGAIN, EVEN AFTER I'VE BEEN STUNG. FORGIVE ME FOR CARING MORE ABOUT PROTECTING MYSELF FROM REAL OR IMAGINED PAIN THAN ABOUT SHOWING YOUR LOVE TO OTHERS.

For all have sinned; all fall short of God's glorious standard.
Romans 3:23

THE DAY WE SPOOKED THE OLD SPANIARD

Dr. Townsend, founder of Wycliffe Bible Translators, pulled a New Testament from his shirt pocket and handed it to the Catholic priest.

"Bishop, would you read some Scripture for us?" he said.

"¡Cómo no, don Guillermo! I'd be happy to," the bishop replied. We were sitting on the front porch of *don Pepe's* ranch house, back in the Lacandon Jungle. The year was 1968. I was flying Dr. Townsend and the local Catholic bishop from village to village on a tour of jungle Indians. Dr. Townsend had asked me if he could visit *don Pepe*, an old Spaniard who had befriended him many years before. So I landed on the crude airstrip in *don Pepe's* front yard.

When the bishop opened the New Testament and *don Pepe* realized he was going to have to listen to the Bible, he started to twist and squirm, looking frantically from side to side like a cornered animal. "I think they are calling me down at the corral," he blurted out desperately. (They weren't.)

Clearly this man, who claimed to be a Catholic, was terrified by the thought of having to listen to the Scriptures, even when his own bishop was reading it from a Catholic New Testament bearing the Pope's imprimatur.

But poor *don Pepe* didn't have a chance. Both his old friend, the aging Dr. Townsend, and his own bishop, Father Samuél Ruíz, outranked him. They gently pushed him down in his chair and made him listen—squirming all the while—while the bishop read the Scriptures and prayed.

As I watched the old Spaniard twist and fidget, I was at first perplexed. "I know I've seen that very same squirming body language before," I puzzled. But I couldn't remember where. Then, as I scoured my memory, it suddenly came to me. I'd seen men act just like that in the little rural Baptist church in Arkansas where my parents took me as a child. Those men would bring their families to church, but stay outside talking, smoking and whittling while the women and children, plus a few old men, did the "religious stuff" inside.

When the annual revival meetings came around, the wives would coax their husbands into the church. During the altar call I saw men struggle so desperately against going forward that their knuckles turned white as they gripped the bench in front of them, squirming and looking around frantically for a way to escape.

What different worlds they lived in—that old Catholic Spanish rancher down in the tropical jungle and those Protestant hardscrabble, depression-era farmers in Arkansas. Yet how very much the same they were under the skin; each of them absolutely terrified at the thought of releasing any control of his life to God.

When I first arrived there in the mountains of southern Mexico a dozen years earlier, it would have been unthinkable for a Catholic bishop and Protestant mission leader to be traveling around together. Local priests used to tell the Indians that we *evangélicos* (Protestants) had tails and ate babies. Several priests lived openly with a mistress. It was a medieval brand of Catholicism, little changed since the sixteenth century. Then the new young bishop, Father Samuél Ruíz, arrived to overturn tradition in our area.

And overturn tradition he did. My wife and I listened in amazement as a Spanish Jesuit stood before a gathering of priests, nuns and upper-class Catholic families while he dramatically proclaimed that all of their religious ceremonies and traditions "can't even be compared in importance with the Bible." (His exact passionate words in Spanish still ring in my ears.) Another priest, with tears streaming down his face, begged his Indian parishioners to forgive the Church for failing them through the centuries.

We gathered around tables in a big room in the Catholic cathedral for Bible study in small groups—using Protestant Bibles —while from the walls all around us 30 dark, life-size oil paintings of former Spanish bishops in full regalia scowled down upon us. ("I wonder what those bishops are thinking?" one of the Catholics in my group snickered.) It was truly a mind-blowing time for this poor Baptist sharecropper's kid from Arkansas.

Dr. Townsend and the old Spaniard have since passed away, but Father Samuél Ruíz is still bishop there in the Chiapas highlands. He is also the mediator between the ski-masked Zapatista rebels and the

Mexican government. I see his name often in the international press these days. Mexican landowners and politicians who oppress the Indians hate the bishop with a passion and have unsuccessfully tried to lobby the Pope to have him removed.

In the meantime, many of the Indians in that area who formerly lived in terror of vengeful spirits have become true Catholics. And even more of them—at least 100,000—have become Protestant *evangélicos*.

LORD, OUR CULTURES AND RELIGIONS ARE SO DIFFERENT, YET HOW VERY MUCH THE SAME WE ARE UNDER THE SKIN. EQUALLY SINFUL, YET EACH OF INFINITE WORTH TO YOU. THANK YOU FOR FORGIVING ME.

*If any of you wants to be my follower, you must put aside your selfish
ambition, shoulder your cross, and follow me.*
Matthew 16:24

THIS TIME WE WON'T
CHASE YOU AWAY

The Muslim elder in long white robe stood before the
crowd of village men as he loudly welcomed me. "If you
want to build a clinic here, this time we won't chase you away.
You can even build a big church if you wish."

"You should have stayed in my house last night," he declared. "I
would have fed you very well." When he finished his speech another
robed elder stood up and repeated the welcome with even more
enthusiasm.

We had bounced for 13 hours over rocky footpaths in a pickup truck
to reach the town of Songe *(Sohn-gay)*, deep in Tanzania, East Africa.
Many years ago some missionaries had tried to build a clinic in that same
village, but they had been driven away by the local Muslims.

But this was 1996. Tanzania's 30-year experiment with socialism had
failed miserably, leaving the people poorer than ever. They had lost all
confidence in their government. Nor had their oil-rich Muslim brothers in
the Middle East helped them either. So these Muslim elders had apparently concluded that the only people who might be willing to help them
were Christians.

Songe lies along the dividing line between the Muslim coastal region
of East Africa and the predominantly Christian interior. Many years ago,
when the two robed elders were only teenagers, one of their friends had
become a Christian. His parents disowned him and the village drove him
out, but he went on to become a pastor and eventually the beloved first
African bishop of the Evangelical Anglican Church in that region. Now
the two Muslim elders talked fondly to us about their former childhood
friend, the bishop. Clearly, their attitude toward Christians had changed.
And much of that change was due to the work and witness of Julias
Mukunda.

Four years before my visit to Songe, Julias and his bride arrived in that then-hostile village. In those four short years this amazing couple had already managed to start six new churches, four of them made up of Muslim converts and two others made up of colorful, nomadic Maasai cattle herders. In order to preach to the Maasai, Julias first had to learn their language. It is as different from his native Swahili as Chinese is from English, but he now speaks Maasai fluently. (He also speaks English, and he has a theological degree.)

What joy on the faces and what enthusiasm in the singing as we worshipped with one of the new congregations in a mud-brick church on the edge of the village. Then we drove up in the hills to a mud-roofed Maasai church where every woman wore a robe of brilliant blue and the men were all dressed in red. During the worship service they danced and chanted their praise to God in traditional Maasai fashion..

Not only is Julias winning people to Christ from among the Maasai, who follow a traditional African religion, he is also winning converts and starting churches among the normally resistant Muslims. In the Middle East and North Africa, Muslim converts to Christianity are rare. But in East Africa, Indonesia and elsewhere, thousands of followers of Islam are turning to Christ these days.

The struggle with Islam is never won through theological debates and arguments, rather through acts of kindness, patience, friendship and love. And it's being won by unsung heroes like Julias Mukunda—talented people who have put aside personal ambitions, shouldered their cross, and buried themselves in out-of-the-way places in order to follow their Lord.

LORD, THANK YOU FOR JULIAS MUKUNDA AND MANY OTHERS LIKE HIM WHO ARE SHOWING YOUR LOVE TO MUSLIMS. THEY WORK IN SUCH HARD PLACES, LORD. ENCOURAGE THEM, I PRAY.

*Jews and Gentiles are the same in this respect. They all have the
same Lord, who generously gives his riches to all who ask for them.*
Romans 10:12

SPOTTING SPUTNIK

A s we gazed up at the Milky Way stretching across a blue-
black moonless sky, the Mayan peasants pointed out a
little metal globe that swept by a hundred miles over our
heads every hour and a half.

This was back in 1957, less than a week after the USSR launched
their *Sputnik*. Those supposedly simple villagers had already spotted that
tiny moving speck in the night sky. And they knew exactly what it was. It
was the first and smallest of all man-made satellites, only the size of a
basketball, but to this day it is the only artificial satellite I have seen with
my own eyes.

I was spending the night in the village of Chan Kom, in the center of
Mexico's Yucatan peninsula . . . no roads, no radios, no electricity, just
one-room thatched roof huts and simple people whose only farming tools
were *machetes* to clear the brush, and pointed sticks to make holes in the
earth to plant their corn and beans. Yet they were experts in astronomy.

In our technology-obsessed culture it's easy to assume that we are
more intelligent than the "simple" peoples of our world. But not so.
God has distributed intelligence rather evenly among all peoples.
Even the most primitive tribes have their geniuses. All cultures are
extremely complex, including those that—unlike ours—give low
priority to machines and buildings. Certainly we have more technical
information, but information is not intelligence. Formal education is
not wisdom.

While Europe was still in the "dark ages," the ancestors of my Mayan
friends were already using a calendar more accurate than ours today.
They could correctly calculate the timing of solar eclipses 10,000 years
into the past and future. They also understood the mathematical concept
of zero, something that eluded the sophisticated Romans. The Mayas
built the pyramids and the amazing astronomical observatory of Chichen
Itzá, whose ruins lie only a dozen miles from the village where their
descendants showed me *Sputnik*. Today, thousands of people come from

all over the world to visit those ruins but pay scant attention to the descendants of their builders who still live nearby.

As I've traveled the remote corners of Planet Earth, I've learned that the United States or the Western World doesn't have an edge on commitment . . . or leadership skills . . . or spirituality . . . or wisdom. In fact, some of the most truly wise people I've met had almost no formal schooling at all, and some of the most obviously spiritual Christians I've met could barely read their Bibles.

I've been privileged and honored to work with hundreds of highly intelligent Christians from many nations and cultures, and I continue to do so today. Some of them have fine academic educations. Most of them do not, but they are no less intelligent. They understand their own people and the subtleties of their language and culture, so they are able to communicate the reality of God's Word to their people far better than I ever could. That's the beauty of partnership in Christ—sharing what each of us does best to get the job done.

The Scriptures say: *The same Lord generously gives his riches to all.* How ridiculous I must seem to God when I equate my knowledge about machines and technical things with superior intelligence or, even worse, when I assume it means I am somehow more spiritual.

I'll never forget the booming voice of the late Rev. Makanzu—a gifted evangelist in French-speaking Africa who made Billy Graham seem dull by comparison—as he said to me, "God has given you Americans the gift of technology, and we need your gift. But God has given us Africans the gift of *heart,* and you need our gift, too."

LORD, HELP ME TO SEE PEOPLE OF OTHER CULTURES AS YOU SEE THEM, WITH ALL THE INCREDIBLE RANGE OF GIFTS YOU HAVE GIVEN THEM.

*Then he put a little child among them. Taking the child in his arms,
he said to them, "Anyone who welcomes a little child like this
one on my behalf welcomes me."*
Mark 9:36-37

CHILDREN OF CHILDREN

S he held her shriveled infant right up to my face and
pleaded for my help as I stood there among 10,000
starving people in the famine camp of Alamata in Ethiopia.

I didn't understand her words, but I didn't need to. I wanted desperately to help her, but there was nothing I could do except point her to the long line of people waiting to be registered.

A few minutes later another mother shoved her emaciated baby in my face as she also pleaded for help. Then another did the same. And another. And another. I felt incredibly frustrated and helpless. I wanted to do something—*anything*—to ease their suffering.

At first I focused my attention on the children and barely looked at the mothers, who seemed drab and middle-aged—just colorless backdrop in a scene of horror. After a while I started looking at the faces of the mothers, too. I still remember the chill I felt when I discovered they were only children, perhaps 12 or 14 years old—younger than my youngest daughter who was then in high school.

Mere children, pleading for the lives of their own children!

That was back in 1985, in a feeding camp among the Tigray people of northern Ethiopia. Tigray parents pledge their daughters in marriage around age nine; sometimes even at birth. At the onset of puberty the marriage is consummated and babies soon follow. That same pattern is common in many other cultures around the world as well.

Every single day about 35,000 children die from malnutrition, childhood diseases and war. Many, if not most, are children of teenage mothers. "Why do those young women keep having babies if they can't feed them?" you may ask. I've even heard American Christians say, "Why should our government give them aid if they're just going to breed like rabbits?"

Do these cynics really think those young mothers have a choice?

More than half of all marriages in our world today are still arranged by parents. Those young mothers in Ethiopia had no voice in who they married or when. Birth control devices were totally beyond their reach. Refusing intercourse with their husbands would bring beatings or death.

And that's the way things are for at least *half of all women on earth today.* They simply have little control over their own bodies.

Not all Third-World cultures marry their daughters off at age nine, of course. Some are more considerate. But other cultures are even worse than the Tigray of Ethiopia. In Thailand, Burma and Cambodia, tens of thousands of poor families *sell their daughters to brothels* as early as age nine or ten. And thousands of men from Europe, Japan and America fly there on sex tours to use their young bodies—sex tours that are advertised on the Internet and winked at by corrupt local officials.

Ironically, the children of these child victims of the sex industry rarely die from disease and malnutrition. That's because their young mothers are usually forced to abort them before they are ever born.

In too many corners of our world today—and even here in my own country—too many children are suffering and dying because of the sins of adults. Sometimes it's the sins of their parents, sometimes those of sexual predators, and often the sins of power hungry political and military leaders who never give a thought to the children.

If *my* heart is broken by all the suffering children and adolescent mothers I have seen, how much more must God's be? He who held them in his arms and blessed them.

LORD, I SIMPLY DON'T UNDERSTAND WHY THERE'S SO MUCH EVIL AND HURT IN OUR WORLD. BUT HELP ME TO AT LEAST DO WHAT I CAN TO HELP SUFFERING CHILDREN . . . AND THEIR CHILDREN!

*Stop judging others, and you will not be judged. For others
will treat you as you treat them.*
Matthew 7:1, 2

TEASING THE DEATH ANGEL

I wasn't surprised when I heard Fred had died in a plane
crash. I knew he had already cheated death more times
than any of us deserves. His other friends knew it, too. In fact,
the cable that informed me of his fatal accident began,
"WELL IT FINALLY HAPPENED."

Fred was a missionary in the Yucatan. His escapades in small
airplanes were known to all the pilots in the region. He took so many
chances that it made me wonder if he had a death wish. But, I'll
always be indebted to Fred for a lesson he taught me about people.

Fred would have made a magnificent politician. Once when he
and I entered a Mexican government office, Fred recognized the man
in charge as an old friend. He grabbed the man's hand in both of his,
looked him straight in the eye and said, "It's good to see you, my
friend. You are looking GREAT!"

"Actually I don't feel very well," the man replied. "In fact, I've
been on sick leave for a year and I only returned to work last week."

Fred never hesitated. "Now that you mention it, you *don't* look
very well," he exclaimed, still looking the man straight in the eye.
"In fact, I can definitely see you have been ill."

The man loved it! As for me, I bit my lips and turned aside to
keep from laughing. Obviously I don't have the stuff of politicians.

Fred's first airplane was a little Piper Super Cub with a big engine
and large tires that allowed him to land just about anywhere. It had no
radio navigational devices and no landing light. But who needs radios
when you have charisma?

One time Fred ran out of fuel while flying above clouds over
central Mexico. Unsure of where he was, he spiraled down through
the clouds and landed on a plowed field. It happened to be near a
Mexican Air Force base. The military had been following him on
radar and sent troops to arrest him, but Fred turned on his charm and
they gave him, instead, a tour of their base, while two dozen soldiers

literally carried his little airplane across the field and over the fence to a highway. There they filled his fuel tank and stopped traffic while he took off and proceeded on his way.

Fred commuted by airplane between his office in the city of Merida and his home in a picturesque Mayan village near the famous ruins of Chichen Itzá. Thick, ground-hugging fog often blankets the area in the morning. Fred would fly above the fog to the big international airport at Merida, where only the tops of the radio towers protruded above the fog. Using the towers to orient himself, he would slow his little plane into landing altitude and descend blind through the thick blanket of fog until he touched down on the wide runway. This was incredibly dangerous and strictly illegal, but he did it again and again. Even today only a few late-model airliners are equipped to land in solid fog like that. And Fred had no electronic landing devices at all. Airport officials shook their heads in disbelief, but they liked Fred too much to report him.

Once when Fred couldn't locate his original destination and night overtook him, he flew along the coast in the dark until he finally reached a town with a lighted runway. Just as he arrived overhead, his fuel ran out. Some men working on an airplane below heard his engine stop. At that very moment a massive power failure blacked out the entire city and airport. Fred could only make out the glow of the surf along the shore. To avoid hitting houses he headed for an area where he remembered some sand dunes.

The men below jumped in a car and followed Fred's wingtip lights as he glided to a certain crash. To their amazement, they found him sitting in his undamaged airplane. He had made a perfect landing on the side of a sand dune in pitch darkness. Tree stumps and logs were lying all around the airplane, but he had missed them all. The men bought Fred a steak dinner to celebrate the miracle.

Another time, Fred became trapped above clouds by a cold front, uncertain whether he was over mountains or the coastal plain. Flying blind, he descended slowly for the next half hour, expecting to smash into the side of a mountain at any second. True to form, his over-worked guardian angel caused him to break out of the low clouds just above the ground . . . right at the base of the mountains and perfectly lined up over a dirt road, on which he immediately landed.

Part of the tiny airstrip at Fred's home village had been dyna-mited out of a solid limestone ridge. In the touchdown area the tips of his wings came within ten feet of solid rock on both sides. The village had no electricity and Fred often arrived after dark. His Mayan helpers were trained to place flashlights along the runway and crank up a little generator to flood the rocks with light. More than once I watched his tiny airplane appear out of the darkness like a phantom, right above the trees, and touch down between the rocky ledges. It was an insane but awesome sight.

One night a sudden storm blocked Fred's route home. He became lost in the darkness and the inevitable fatal crash finally occurred.

I abhorred Fred's flying practices. Nevertheless, I learned a lesson from him that changed my perspective for life. It happened after I landed on a new airstrip at an isolated interior village. I knew Fred had landed there before, so I wasn't concerned about the condition of the runway. As I touched down I found the runway not only ran uphill but was so rough I thought it might shake my airplane to pieces.

The local believers rushed up to greet me and ask me what I thought of their new airstrip. In good direct American fashion I told them it was the worst place I had ever landed and they would have to do a lot more work to improve it. I went on to elaborate on all the faults of their handiwork. In fact, I was so intent on teaching them the "proper" standards for an airstrip that I barely noticed how their faces dropped in disappointment.

Fred flew in that afternoon and we spent the night in the village. That evening he casually said to me, "The brothers tell me you aren't too happy with their airstrip." "Of course not," I replied. "It felt like I was landing up the steps of the Capitol building in Washington. It's the worst place I've ever landed!"

There was a quiet sadness in Fred's eyes. I think he shook his head ever so slightly as he softly replied, "And I had already told them how wonderful it is."

I felt like a knife had gone through me. I had been so set on telling those people how to do things the right way—*my way*—that I never gave a thought to *their* feelings.

Fred, on the other hand, was thinking about all the weeks those new Christians had labored out in the searing sun and steaming heat with simple hand tools to hack the airstrip of virgin jungle, neglecting their own crops to do so. All that work just to make it easy for us to visit them and tell them more about Jesus.

That night I learned the true meaning of the Golden Rule. It's a lesson I hope I never forget.

LORD, PLEASE HELP ME NOT TO CRITICIZE OTHERS UNLESS I HAVE WALKED LONG IN THEIR SANDALS.

> *Greet all the brothers with a holy kiss.*
> *I Thessalonians 5:26 (NIV)*

HAND IN HAND WITH JOSÉ

My first impulse was to slug him when he took me by the arm and continued to hold it as we walked along. Everything in my upbringing had taught me to interpret his action as a sexual advance.

"Hold it!" I said to myself, "you know this man too well. Think this through before you do something rash."

I was walking down the street in Mexico City with my good friend José. We lived far apart and saw each other only rarely, but each time our paths crossed we would talk far into the night, discussing our personal pilgrimages and sharing our personal dreams. José had studied in Switzerland and the United States. He understood my background as none of my other Mexican friends did. He was an ordained minister and a deeply spiritual Christian. In some ways he was my spiritual model.

This happened years ago, before it was common for men in our culture to embrace, or for winning sports teams to hug each other and dance around together. A generation ago most American men touched only for a handshake or a slap on the back.

As we walked along, José continued to hold me by the arm while I fought a raging battle within. I was reacting as a product of my culture and he of his. He was saying, "I'm your friend." Nothing more. But I was hearing something very different indeed.

* * * * *

Since that afternoon long ago I have traveled far. In places as different as Asia, Africa and among Indians in the Amazon, I have seen young men holding hands in friendship. And friendship is all it is. Apparently not all cultures are as sex-obsessed as ours seems to be.

When I hear Chinese spoken, I know immediately that I don't understand what is being said. We all know how different spoken languages can be, but it's easy to assume that *body language* is everywhere the same. Actually, body languages in other cultures can be as different from ours as English from Chinese, only the differences are not so readily apparent.

Most American businessmen, for example, are absolutely convinced they can judge a person's character by the firmness of his handshake and the way he looks you straight in the eye. But many cultures show respect by looking down. For them, direct eye contact is the height of impudence. So the businessman may conclude that the person is devious or spineless when, in fact, he or she may only be showing respect.

In some cultures a loud burp means, "Thank you for that excellent meal!" In ours . . . well, it has a somewhat *different* meaning.

In Ethiopia, a polite host takes food in his hand and stuffs it into the mouth of an honored guest. In our culture, hardly anything could be considered more rude.

In France and Russia, as we are all aware, men greet each other with ceremonial kisses on the cheek.

And in some cultures men hold hands simply because they are friends.

I learned many things from my good friend José. That afternoon I learned not to jump to conclusions.

LORD, HELP ME TO ASSUME THE BEST—NOT THE WORST—IN OTHERS, UNTIL I HAVE CLEAR REASON TO DO OTHERWISE.

Michal, the daughter of Saul, looked down from her window.
When she saw King David leaping and dancing before the Lord,
she was filled with contempt for him.
2 Samuel 6:16

EMOTIONAL ABOUT EMOTION

"I don't believe there is ANY PLACE in the Christian life for EMOTION!" My missionary friend's face was blazing red and his tightly clenched fist pounded the table between us to accentuate every word as he spoke. He could hardly have been more emotional.

I still want to burst out laughing every time I remember that ironic scene. My friend did have reason to be emotional. From his perspective, everything he had worked and sacrificed for over the past 20 years was being threatened.

Presbyterian missionaries were the first protestants to enter the country of Colombia back in the nineteenth century. They founded outstanding schools and hospitals, plus a handful of churches in the larger cities. The churches were led by Colombian pastors who were well educated but few in number. The Synod of Colombia had also tried to start churches in the rough-and-tumble rural northwestern part of the country, but with minimal success.

American missionaries—my red-faced friend among them— worked extremely hard to plant churches in the Northwest. Several different families of missionaries lived in remote villages, traveled widely by horseback, preached, treated the sick, improved the crops, and poured out their lives for the people there. After nearly 30 years of effort, the missionaries had only two churches and eight or ten preaching points to show for all their years of hard work and sacrifice.

I had been invited there by the National Presbyterian Synod of Colombia to help them to increase the growth of churches in that backward region.

We traveled by horseback and jeep throughout the rugged mountains—then as now home to Marxist guerrilla bands—to visit the churches and preaching points. We talked with the missionaries and we met two impressive Colombian lay pastors. In the process, we also learned about an independent church movement in a neighboring area that was growing very rapidly.

I merely suggested to the Presbyterians that they should develop closer ties with the other movement and learn from its success. That's when my friend exploded in his red-faced, emotional tirade against emotion. You see, the other movement was mildly charismatic in doctrine. They weren't even true Pentecostals, but they did hold faith healing services. Any charismatic expression at all was simply too threatening for this "nonemotional" missionary.

In spite of this man's negative reaction, the national leaders of the Colombian Church agreed to seek ties with the other movement. They also accepted my recommendation that they should ordain their two rural lay pastors without requiring seminary training.

Educated Colombian city pastors simply would not serve in primitive rural areas, whereas the two lay pastors had grown up in the Northwest and were happy to live there. They had already amply demonstrated their maturity and leadership ability and they had sufficient training to serve their unsophisticated congregations.

Before our visit, the foreign missionaries were the only ordained persons living in the Northwest, so only they could lead in celebrating the sacraments. Apparently it had never occurred to them that this gave a decidedly foreign image to the Gospel, and that it may have kept people away. After the local lay pastors were ordained, they led the sacraments, demonstrating to their people that theirs was not a "foreign" religion after all.

Such a small change, but what a difference it made.

Five years later, when we went back for a review, we found to our delight—but not surprise—that the Presbyterian movement had grown four or five times as much in that short period as in 30 previous years. The Gospel had *finally* taken root in the unsophisticated culture of the rural Northwest.

*   *   *   *   *

King David was so caught up in praising his Lord that he never gave a thought to his dignity. Michal, on the other hand, was all wrapped up in her own pride and her husband's image. It's easy to smile at my missionary brother's fear of emotional expression in his faith, but I have to confess that I'm a lot like him—more like Michal than David. In fact, I've become rather skilled at avoiding situations where I might be embarrassed or look ridiculous.

LORD, HELP ME TO LOOSEN UP. EVEN BE WILLING TO LOOK RIDICULOUS FOR YOU.

We depend on the Lord alone to save us.
Only he can help us, protecting us like a shield.
Psalm 33:20

DIVING WITH ALLIGATORS

I must have looked pretty ridiculous with a five-gallon paint can over my head. The long-haired Lacandon men in bark cloth robes circled us with their dugout canoes, whooping with laughter and pointing at me as I donned the crude diving helmet and slipped over the side of our canoe into the murky waters of Lake Najá.

My companion played out the air hose of our portable air compressor as I descended into the black depths, praying that the alligators that lived around the edges wouldn't swim out in the middle of the lake. The last of my air hose was stretched tightly over the edge of the canoe when my feet finally settled into the soft mud bottom 60 feet below.

An adventure photographer had accidentally dropped an expensive movie camera on a tripod into the lake while he was filming from a canoe. He marked the spot and told me I was welcome to the camera if I could find it. For me, a 23-year-old novice missionary pilot, finding the camera was more than just an adventure. It was worth at least two years of my $70-per-month salary.

I calculated what the water pressure would be at 60 feet and confirmed that our little portable air compressor could handle it. So I riveted a plastic faceplate on the side of a large paint can, brazed an air hose fitting into the top, and *voilà*—a diving helmet. I convinced a friend to go along to man the compressor, flew out to a tiny airstrip next to the lake, and down I went.

Unfortunately, our rock anchor stirred up the ooze on the bottom, so my visibility was zero. I wandered around in total darkness for about 15 minutes, vainly thinking I might step on the camera or its large tripod. I finally realized the situation was hopeless and slowly rose to the surface. There the Lacandon men were no longer laughing. In fact, they were oohing and aahing, highly impressed that I could stay under water that long.

The Lacandons are true jungle dwellers, descendants of the ancient Mayan civilization. They still hunt and fish with bows and arrows. From clay they fashion crude "god-pots" in which they burn pine-pitch incense to appease the spirits. The men make pilgrimages to ruined Mayan cities deep in the jungle to worship the gods of their ancestors.

When Phil and Mary Baer trekked into the Lacandon jungle in the late 1940s, they found only about 200 of these people left, living in three widely separated villages. Marriage partners were so limited that men sometimes married their own sisters. Inbreeding was taking its toll. Few children were being born and fewer survived infancy. Genetic defects were common. Custom required that when a man visited a Lacandon home, his host must offer him his wife for the night, so venereal disease was also rampant. The Lacandons were a dispirited, dying culture when this fearless missionary couple reached them half a century ago.

Before the mission plane service began, Mary Baer and the children would remain in Najá alone during one week of each month while Phil hiked three days to the nearest Mexican town to buy supplies, then three days back with all the supplies he could carry on his back. Even after Phil hacked a tiny airstrip out of the jungle so basic supplies could be flown in, life was still lonely and hard in their crude little house made of hand-hewn slabs of solid mahogany. After several years in Najá, Mary and Phil pulled up stakes and repeated the process among the other two groups of Lacandons.

Little by little the Baers won the trust of the suspicious Lacandons. They healed their sores, kept visitors from exploiting them, learned their language and customs, translated the New Testament, taught them to read, and told them about the God who loves them.

The old *shaman,* keeper of tribal magic, controlled his people with fear, so Mary and Phil saw no Christian converts for several years. But they began to notice that more children were being born and surviving. Slowly, the number of Lacandons crept up to about 250. A dying people had been saved from extinction, at least for another generation. In the process several were saved spiritually as well.

Phil and Mary were away on furlough when I made my dive to

the bottom of Lake Najá, and their mahogany house was tightly locked. By the time I surfaced, a cold wind was blowing and it had started to rain. Clouds completely blanketed the area, blocking any possibility of flying out. We were wet and cold and we hadn't come prepared to spend the night. The Indians had long since gone to their huts back in the jungle. Shivering all night in the airplane wasn't very appealing, so we foolishly decided to walk three or four miles over a muddy jungle trail to a village of Tzeltal Indians (a different tribe) where a family of missionary Bible translators was living.

Neither my companion nor I had been over that trail before, but I had once buzzed low over the Tzeltal village to drop medicines by parachute, so I knew the lay of the surrounding cliffs. We trudged along through the muddy jungle until, just at twilight, we came to a fork in the trail. Which way to go? We knew if we took the wrong trail the nearest village was a dozen miles away. My companion said, "I think it's this way." I looked up at the cliffs and said, "I think it's that way." Fortunately, I was right. With barking dogs announcing our arrival, we appeared well after dark, wet and freezing, at the door of the surprised missionaries in the middle of the jungle.

You've heard the saying, "God looks after children and fools." He was certainly watching over us that evening, in spite of our foolish presumption. We were in treacherous country. Only a couple of weeks later, that very same missionary translator left his village with his eight-year-old son to go hunting nearby. They stepped a few yards off the trail, became disoriented, and wandered among jungle-covered limestone sinkholes for three days and nights while all the men of the village and two small airplanes overhead searched for them. The boy was unconscious when they were finally found, but he survived.

I confess that I don't know why God protects some of us when we do dumb things, but I am grateful. I'm also grateful for intrepid Christian missionaries like Phil and Mary who are taking deliberate risks for something far more valuable than a movie camera, for the lives and souls of people who have never heard the Good News about God's love. These days more of those missionaries come from the Third World than from Europe and America.

Meanwhile, deep in the muck, 60 feet below the surface of a tiny jungle lake in Mexico, an expensive movie camera still waits for someone to find it. Want to give it a try?

*THANK YOU FOR PROTECTING ME, LORD. HELP ME TO LAY ALL
THAT I AM ON YOUR ALTAR AND FOLLOW YOU TODAY.*

Ethiopia famine camp where young mothers confronted the author. (Page 44)

Chatting with Lacandon men in barkcloth robes. (Page 55)

Ancient Omec ruins discovered by the author. (Page 77)

A leper in the village where there was beauty amid despair. (Page 8)

*And everyone will know that the LORD does not need weapons to rescue
his people. It is his battle, not ours. The Lord will give you to us.*
I Samuel 17:47

DAVID AND GOLIATH IN THE DESERT

"The French Officers begged us not to try it, but we said,
if we die, we die!'"

I listened with fascination as the general described in animated detail
how his troops had defeated Mohamar Khadaffi's Libyan army only a
few days earlier. The general and I were dinner guests in the home of a
mutual friend in Ndjamena, Chad.

Chad is one of the poorest, least-developed countries on earth. It's
twice as big as France but has only 50 miles of paved road. Its only
"industries" are a brewery and a few cotton gins. Ndjamena, the capital,
is more like a large village than a city.

Khadaffi's Libyan troops then occupied the northern half of Chad—
all desert. To protect their former colony, the French had sent in their air
force and drawn a line in the sand—so to speak—to keep the Libyans
from advancing even farther. In occupied territory the Libyans built two
air bases, surrounded by vast mine fields and armed with the latest Soviet
equipment—MIG jet fighters, tanks, helicopter gunships and radar.
Against all that sophisticated weaponry the Chadians had only machine
guns mounted on Toyota four-wheel-drive pickup trucks.

The general's voice swelled with excitement and pride as he
described how his desert fighters had captured the two Libyan air bases
inside Chad. At the crack of dawn his daredevils came in from all direc-
tions, driving their Toyotas *straight across the mine fields at about 100
miles per hour,* firing wildly as they came. Their pickups with big desert
tires were so light and moved so fast that they set off only a few of the
land mines.

The sleeping Libyans awoke to sheer pandemonium. Over a thousand
gave up without a fight. When a few Libyans ran off into the surrounding
desert to escape, the Chadians didn't even bother to follow. They simply
waited for them to come straggling back on the third day, happy to
surrender to get water.

The courageous Chadians captured several MIG fighters and helicopter gunships, but they had no pilots to fly them. So they sold them to Saddam Hussein. Some of those same planes may have been shot down over Iraq during the 1991 Middle East war.

No wonder the French liked to use Chadians for soldiers back when Chad was still their colony. They are some of the toughest, bravest men on earth. I never did understand why this story of the Chadian David defeating the Libyan Goliath in the desert received so little coverage in the world press.

The next morning we met with the second-in-command at the Chadian Foreign Ministry. My companion, a Japanese citizen, mentioned that he had good contacts in his own government and offered to encourage foreign aid from Japan to Chad. The Chadian official thanked him politely, then with a sly smile said, "Don't forget to tell your government about Chad's foreign aid to Japan."

Naturally we were intrigued and amused at the thought of one of the world's poorest countries sending foreign aid to one of the richest. And, of course, we asked him to explain, as he clearly wanted us to do.

"You have heard how our troops captured those Libyan air bases? Well, we also captured dozens of Toyota trucks from the Libyans. Khadaffi will have to order replacements from Japan." He smiled triumphantly. "So that's our contribution to the Japanese economy!"

*   *   *   *   *

But why have I put a war story in a book like this one? Because the unequal battle between the Chadians and Libyans reminds me of another kind of battle that is taking place in out-of-the-way places all around our world today—the battle for the hearts and souls of men and women.

This battle for hearts and souls is not being won by people with money and computers and university or seminary degrees, but by poor and powerless local Christians in out-of-the-way places who are willing to risk all and throw themselves against impossible odds because of their unstoppable faith.

Isn't that, after all, why we have the story of David and Goliath in the Bible? To remind us that it is "not by might, nor by power, but by my Spirit, says the Lord."

LORD, I THANK YOU FOR ALL THE OPPORTUNITIES AND RESOURCES YOU HAVE GIVEN ME, BUT HELP ME NEVER TO RELY ON THEM INSTEAD OF ON YOU.

*Nothing in all creation can be hid from him. Everything is naked and
exposed before his eyes. This is the God to whom we
must explain all that we have done.*

Hebrews 4:13

GERTRUDE'S SECRET

As we screamed by at nearly 150 miles an hour, the tip of
my right wing was almost scraping the rocky canyon
wall.

Overhead, thick clouds covered the narrow canyon from rim to
rim. To my left another vertical wall of rock boxed us in. In front of
us the canyon twisted and turned. This narrow canyon was my "secret
passage" through the mountain range when clouds and rain did not
allow safe flight over the top.

Most people would have been terrified to fly through that tunnel
of rock, but in the seat next to me Gertrude chattered away nonstop
about how totally unafraid she was—how she had flown through
those mountains many times before.

Suddenly, as we came around a bend in the narrow canyon, I saw
our path ahead blocked by heavy rain. In a flash I throttled back the
engine, pulled on full flaps and flipped us into a tight, gut-twisting
reversing maneuver—a kind of diagonal partial loop followed by half
roll. The canyon simply wasn't wide enough for a normal turn.

For a moment, while G-load smashed us into our seats during the
turn, we seemed to be flying straight at a wall of solid rock. At that
instant I glanced at Gertrude and saw her face filled with absolute
terror, her white-knuckled hands clinging to the leather strap on the
doorpost.

Flying through that rocky crack in a mountain, I had glimpsed a
crack in Gertrude's own rock-hard exterior.

Gertrude was the daughter of a Reformed Church pastor in
Switzerland, but she would have nothing to do with her father's
religion. She was something of a legend in southeast Mexico. People
said she was a Communist; that she had fought in the Spanish Civil
War; that through her political influence a shipload of refugees had
been turned away from Veracruz to certain death. That's what local

Mexican gossips told me. I have no idea how much of it was true.

What I did know was that after she emigrated to Mexico she married a German-American professor who was a renowned expert on the ruins of the ancient Mayas. He died soon after I arrived there.

Gertrude not only talked tough, she looked tough. She always wore khaki pants, safari jacket and rough hiking shoes—garb that was absolutely shocking for a woman in that culture back then. She claimed to be an anthropologist and saw herself as protector of the Lacandons, the long-haired, bark-cloth-clad dwellers of the tropical jungle that still bears their name.

Gertrude detested missionaries and ridiculed them constantly, but she always treated me well, probably to make sure I would be willing to fly her out of the jungle in case the local Mexican bush pilots left her stranded. Anyway, that's why she was riding with me that day.

I never said a word to Gertrude about her display of terror. But I had seen right inside her carefully crafted shell of bravado. *And she knew it!* Never again did she try to snow me with her tough talk. She even volunteered to let me use her late husband's outstanding personal library.

Gertrude's feigned toughness was obvious to most people who knew her—but apparently not to Gertrude herself. Inside, she was just as insecure and frightened as the rest of us. So frightened, in fact, that she covered up by talking tough and never letting down her guard.

Shakespeare was right: *All the world's a stage, and all the men and women merely players.* Each of us goes through life playing to audiences of our own invention. An actor in a theater is acutely aware of his or her audience but, strangely, we on the stage of life are rarely conscious of ours. Nevertheless, our subconscious audience dominates most of our thoughts and actions and often determines the course of our lives.

An uncle of mine was snubbed by his city high-school classmates because he was a poor farm boy. For the next 50 years he lived far away and only returned home four or five times for brief visits. Yet, almost till the day he died he talked about making lots of money and going back to "show them." His former classmates perhaps didn't even remember him but they controlled his life as surely as if they had been sitting on his shoulder.

Perhaps I am not so different from my uncle or Gertrude as I'd like to think. How often do I play my own pathetic games of bravado, fooling myself usually, others sometimes, but God never!

As for Gertrude, they tell me she continued with her facade of false bravery and self-deceit to the end.

LORD, KEEP ME FROM PLAYACTING WITH THE PEOPLE AROUND ME. HELP ME TO HAVE THE COURAGE TO BE GENUINE.

The proud Pharisee stood by himself and prayed this prayer:
'I thank you, God, that I am not a sinner like everyone else, especially
like that tax collector over there!'
Luke 18:11
Don't be selfish; don't live to make a good impression on others.
Be humble, thinking of others as better than yourself.
Philippians 2:3

SAFARI SUIT SYNDROME

"**S**top! Please don't try to duplicate what I have told you," I pleaded. "I don't know your culture. Mexico is not the same as Rhodesia."

It was my very first visit to Africa, back in 1969. The British colony of Rhodesia (now Zimbabwe) had recently declared itself independent under Ian Smith's all-white government. Racial tensions were high.

I had gone to Rhodesia to evaluate our mission airplane service, but somehow communications were scrambled and I had been billed as a visiting church growth expert. A small plane picked me up in the capital and flew me out to a rural school where about 30 African pastors, school headmasters and American missionaries were gathered for their annual men's retreat.

The meeting was already underway. As soon as I walked in the door they introduced me and asked me to immediately speak on the subject of church growth. Talk about being put on the spot!

I had nothing prepared, so I decided to tell them stories about the fast-growing Christian movement in Mexico where I had worked for several years. I recounted some of the mistakes my fellow missionaries and I had made . . . how the churches kept growing anyway, even though they were led mostly by lay volunteers . . . how they often told me, "The best way to ruin a good church is to give it a full-time pastor." I also told them I had learned far more from those humble Christians in Mexico than I had ever taught them.

As I described some of the mistakes we missionaries had made, the Africans were entranced. But I noticed the white American leader of the missionaries in Rhodesia was getting more and more agitated. He was leaning against the back wall and wearing a safari suit, the symbol of white colonialism to the Africans in those racially charged days in white-ruled Rhodesia. Apparently he didn't want to me to tell the Africans that Western missionaries make mistakes. (As if they didn't already know.)

When I finished talking, the Africans began to ask questions.

First question: "The people in that place you call Mexico, are they white or are they black?"

"Actually neither," I replied. "Sort of light brown."

"But they are not white?"

"No," I conceded, "most of them are not white." A sigh of relief passed over their faces.

Next question: "Here in Rhodesia the young people in our churches are starting to rebel against their parents. Do they have that problem in Mexico, and how do they handle it?"

I agreed they did have the same problem and described some of their attempted solutions.

Then they asked another question about a church problem and I again described how the Mexican church handled it.

During my response to their third question, it suddenly hit me! The look in their eyes told me they were going right home to apply everything I told them in their own churches. I concluded that this was the first time these African leaders had heard about churches they could relate to emotionally. Until then they had only heard idealized stories from white missionaries about churches in America and Great Britain.

That's when I begged them not to try to duplicate what I had told them about the churches in Mexico. I didn't want them to replace one culturally inappropriate model with another.

I'll never forget the hunger those African church leaders had for contact with other Third-World Christians. The missionaries had kept them in an isolated cocoon, trying to mold them into carbon copies of churches in America. The Africans wanted to hear about somebody—anybody—who was more like them.

The mission director couldn't have treated me more coldly if icicles had been hanging from his chin. Unwittingly I had challenged his tight little religious empire. I, in turn, couldn't help comparing him in my mind to the proud Pharisee at prayer in the temple.

I'm sure those missionaries in Rhodesia did care about the African people, but most of them nevertheless demonstrated a condescending attitude toward the Africans and seemed quite comfortable with the white-run government. The African pastors and leaders sensed this, and the tension between them and the missionaries was palpable—like electricity in the air.

However, the tension didn't fall strictly along racial lines. A white American pharmacist in the mission hospital clearly enjoyed being with the Africans and they reciprocated by showing him great respect and trust. Some of the Africans even told me how different he was.

All this took place a quarter of a century ago. White colonialism has long since disappeared from Africa. So have most of those missionaries with colonial mentalities. These days missionaries work *under* Africans.

But sometimes attitudes leave long trails. Not long ago I read an article in a mission journal about the danger of trusting Africans. It was written by the *current* field director of that same mission in the same country. Why was I not surprised to note that the writer of the article is the *son* of the icicle-chinned former director, the man I had so offended when I told the Africans that missionaries make mistakes?

It's easy to find fault with pharisaical people like that self-righteous mission field leader, but don't I also sometimes try to create my own comfortable little kingdom? And how clever I am at convincing myself that I am justified in holding on to it.

HELP ME, LORD, TO BE HONEST WITH MYSELF ABOUT MY OWN MOTIVES. AND HELP ME TO HAVE THE COURAGE TO LET GO.

*Now a despised Samaritan came along, and when he saw the man,
he felt deep pity . . . . Now which of these three would you say
was a neighbor to the man . . . ?*
Luke 10:33 & 36

GOD'S MINUTE MAN

"***B****eliever, don't be scandalized by me! Be scandalized by
your own sins!*"

I saw those words on a life-size bronze statue of Jesus on the cross. It
stands in a garden next to a Catholic church in the high, cold city of
Bogotá, Colombia, in a former slum neighborhood called *El Minuto de
Dios* (God's Minute). And the *man* who completely transformed that
former slum was a truly remarkable priest, Father García Herrera.

I met Father García late on a rainy afternoon in 1975. He was clearly
exhausted when we met, but he still exuded kindness and patience.
Colombia is the stronghold of the most conservative, old-style Catholics
in all of Latin America, and Father García came from one of the country's
most powerful traditional families. His poise and graciousness clearly
showed his aristocratic roots, but this unusual priest was anything but
traditional.

With his family connections, García could have chosen a comfortable
parish among the elite. Instead he went to work among the poor in a *barrio*
where filth, alcoholism and violence were the norm. Little by little he gained
the trust of the people and began to convince them of God's love for them.
Under his leadership they cleaned up the garbage-filled streets, built schools
and a new church, and began to replace their shacks with brick and cement
houses. Father García offered money for building loans, but his requirements
were strict—only those who worked hard and pledged to stop all *vicios* like
alcohol and drugs could qualify for house lots and loans. Their neighbors
made sure they kept their pledges.

"God's Minute," the unusual name of the neighborhood, was also the
name of Father García's daily five-minute devotional program on national television. In those days there was only one TV channel in Colombia, so his face and message were well known throughout the country.
His closest associate was a Baptist—a Mexican-American from San
Diego, California, who often filled in for the priest on television. Both
men taught directly from the Scriptures.

To finance his work, once each year García rented the grand ballroom of the Tequendama Hotel, largest in the country, for a fundraising dinner. His guests each paid the present-day equivalent of about 500 U.S. dollars for a "banquet" of the same food Jesus fed the 5,000—a piece of fish, a piece of bread, and a glass of water. They also received a New Testament in simple Spanish. The Catholic hierarchy in Colombia resented and detested Father García, but the Archbishop was nevertheless obliged to attend the annual fundraising dinner because the President of Colombia and most of the elite were always there.

A famous sculptor was so impressed by Father Garcia's ministry that he made the bronze statue of Jesus as a gift, to be placed on the steeple of his church. The statue was naked, as Jesus probably was on the cross. This so scandalized the Catholic hierarchy that they refused to allow Father García to put it on the church. So he placed it in a quiet little garden near the church, together with the words about sin and scandal.

When I met this amazing priest, he had already heard about the fast-growing Protestant church movement in northwest Colombia where I was then working. He listened and asked questions with enthusiasm as I described the movement. As we parted—standing in a cold drizzle by my car—he placed his hand on my shoulder and prayed a warm, spontaneous evangelical prayer that I shall never forget.

In my childhood and youth I had been conditioned to look on Catholics in much the same way the Jews of Jesus' day looked on Samaritans. When I met Father García I'd already lived and traveled in Latin America for 20 years, so I'd met other priests and realized they aren't all alike. But this amazing man overturned all my remaining stereotypes.

And that's really the essence of what I have learned in my journeys to the remote corners of our world—that God simply refuses to conform to my stereotypes.

HOW STRANGE, LORD, THAT I FIND IT EASY TO BELIEVE YOU COULD WORK THROUGH CATHOLIC PRIESTS LIKE MARTIN LUTHER, JOHN CALVIN AND MENNO SIMMONS 450 YEARS AGO, YET SURPRISED THAT YOU CAN DO THE SAME TODAY. FORGIVE ME.

Praise him with a blast of trumpet; praise him with the lyre and harp!
Praise him with the tambourine and dancing; praise him with
stringed instruments and flutes! Praise him with a clash of cymbals;
praise him with loud clanging cymbals. Let everything that
lives sing praises to the LORD!
Psalms 150:3-6

PRAISE THE LORD WITH FIRECRACKERS

Pop! Pop! Pop-pop-pop-pop-pop-pop-pop-pop! Minute after minute the explosions kept going—thousands of them—as two men fed a long belt of firecrackers over the edge of the roof. Smoke from the machine-gun-like explosions obscured the building.

We had gone there to "Red Bridge Village" in southern China to celebrate the completion of a new church building. And what a celebration it was! Firecrackers and singing and speeches, plus a sermon. And mountains of food. Our government-assigned chaperon from the Bureau of Religious Affairs—who had to pledge he had no religion in order to get his job—also gave a speech. I chose my words carefully during my brief remarks, congratulating them for being part of the largest, fastest-growing family on earth—the family of Christians.

The guest preacher from another part of China gave a clear gospel message, then with a sly smile pointed to the government official sitting next to me. "How many of you will promise to pray for this man?" he asked the audience. Every hand in the church shot up. "See! Your life is going to change," he teased the government man, whose face flushed beet red with embarrassment.

In 1984 there had been only one Christian in Red Bridge village. She was a young woman from another area who married a local man and soon won him to Christ. Four years later there were 30 believers in the village. When we visited in 1994, there were 300. And the growth continues. In fact, the number of believers in that local district—or county—grew from 900 to 10,000 during those same ten years.

The woman's first convert, her husband, received training through

Partners International and is now the local pastor. However, I came away with the impression that the wife is really the behind-the-scenes leader of the community.

The speed with which people are turning to Christ in China today boggles the mind. When the Communists took control in 1949—a hundred years after missionaries began work in China—there were less than a million Protestant Christians in all of China, plus about three million Catholics. Today there are almost certainly more than 50 million believers. Some people think there may be 100 million. Outsiders like me are only allowed to visit government registered churches such as the one in Red Bridge village. However, 80 or 90 percent of all churches in China are unregistered, meeting more or less secretly in homes. In some areas local authorities tolerate them. In other areas they are still pursued and persecuted, forced to meet in total secrecy.

Amazingly, God allowed communism to break the hold of the traditional religions and created a deep hunger for meaning in life—a sort of spiritual vacuum that prepared the way for this explosion of church growth.

Before the Communists came to power, each region of China had its own distinct dialect, virtually unintelligible to the others, and only a small percentage of the people could read and write. Mao Tse-Tung imposed Mandarin as the standard language throughout the country and simplified the complex Chinese pictograph writing. Now most people in China understand Mandarin and are able to read and write. This means they are now able to read the Scriptures, making it far easier to evangelize and train local leaders than it ever was before.

Furthermore, about 30 years ago the infamous Red Guard movement scattered Chinese Christians all over the country. Like the early believers described in The Acts of the Apostles, everywhere they went they talked about Jesus.

Virtually all schools in China were closed for several years during the time of the Red Guards. The generation that missed out on schooling is now in its thirties and forties. Desperate to make up for what they missed, they are some of the most highly motivated students in the world.

This frantic search for learning makes an entire generation more open to the gospel message, but equally open to other religions. Cults and sects abound. One pseudo-Christian sect blanketed the cities with millions of leaflets, urging people to oppose the government and claiming their leader is Jesus returned to earth. Not surprisingly, the government then cracked down on *all* Christians.

Tens of thousands of house churches are led by lay men and women in their twenties. Entire "networks" (quasi-denominations), made up of several thousand house churches have not a single seminary-trained pastor.

These Chinese believers already know how to evangelize effectively. Their great need is for appropriate on-the-job training in Bible and leadership for thousands of local church lay leaders. But it must be on their terms. They insist that the training must be appropriate to their culture and their present political situation. Translations of training materials from the West—or even from Taiwan—are rarely effective. They simply don't fit the reality of life inside China today. So the house church leaders in China are now producing most of their own training materials.

It seems like it was only yesterday when I, like most Christians in the West, pretty much gave up on China. We thought a hundred years of missionary work and sacrifice had been lost—that Christianity had all but disappeared inside the hermetically sealed land of Mao's Little Red Book, Red Guards and "Great Leap Forward." The situation seemed so hopeless that most of us even stopped praying for China.

Who could have believed that only 20 years later China would be experiencing the most rapid numerical growth of the Christian faith of any nation in history? But that's what happened.

How like God to cause even the wrath of arrogant men like Mao Tse-Tung to praise him.

FORGIVE ME, LORD, FOR FAILING TO BELIEVE THAT YOU ARE ALWAYS IN CONTROL, EVEN WHEN THINGS SEEM HOPELESS.

Fools think they need no advice, but the wise listen to others.
Proverbs 12:15
Plans go wrong for lack of advice; many counselors bring success.
Proverbs 15:22

THE GOSPEL CABIN CRUISER

They showed up right after the first road was opened through the swamps into our town—two American men and a woman, towing a large cabin-cruiser boat behind their car.

Someone had given one of the men the cabin cruiser as a totally unexpected gift. He saw it as a sign from God. He decided that God must have given him the boat to use to find lost Indian tribes. So he and his friends towed the boat all the way from their home in Michigan to southeast Mexico.

The trio spoke no Spanish but they had happily "evangelized" along the way by tossing gospel tracts wrapped in colored cellophane from their car windows. A large sign on the back of the boat proclaimed the word "Jesus." I didn't have the heart to tell them that *"Jesús"* was the common name for a dog or beggar in that culture.

The trio proudly showed us their collection of gospel records in the languages of several Indian tribes of Mexico. (One was actually a Christmas record in Spanish, but they thought *Navidad* was the name of a tribe.) They planned to travel along the rivers in their boat, stopping at each house or village to play different records until they found one their listeners understood. Their enthusiasm was undaunted when I told them I was sure there were no lost Indian tribes—that I knew every village in the state and 200 of them already had evangelical churches.

They agreed with us that it would be good if they could learn to speak Spanish. Unfortunately, they just didn't have time because spreading the Gospel was too urgent.

The trio launched their boat in the wide Grijalva River and soon disappeared from sight. Four days later they were back. They found no Indians, but they did somehow end up in the Gulf of Mexico, after failing to see the entrance to the half-mile-wide Usumacinta River.

One man was barefoot. (His shoes fell overboard.) The woman was an emotional wreck. They'd all had enough.

I couldn't help thinking of Joe Bayly's hilarious book, *The Gospel Blimp,* in which a man and his friends try to evangelize the next-door neighbor by purchasing a blimp and dropping gospel tracts into his yard. We breathed a big sigh of relief as we watched the boat with its Jesus sign heading north, sure we had seen the last of this well-intentioned but incredibly naive trio.

How wrong we were!

Two years later the same two men, towing the same cabin cruiser, appeared once again at our door. (This time the wife stayed home.) Month after month they had been driving the back roads of the American Southwest and northern Mexico, dragging their boat behind them and searching for a place where they could use it to spread the Gospel. They told us they did find a big lake behind a new government dam in northwest Mexico. Unfortunately, no people lived on the lake. Reluctantly, they concluded that our area was the only part of Mexico that had enough rivers.

This time I knew it was pointless to try to dissuade them, so I showed them an area on their maps where there were several rivers and no churches. (Of course there were no people there either, except five or six houses I had spotted from the air.) They were ecstatic over the information I had given them, and off they went again to find lost Indians.

Half way across a wide lagoon that led to the mouths of the rivers, their engine stopped. (After all, it had been sitting unused on its trailer for several months.) As they worked to restart the engine, a vicious cold front swept in from the Gulf of Mexico. Waves in the shallow lagoon grew higher and higher and Mexican fishing boats all headed for shore. A sympathetic boat captain offered to tow them to port. Like "the gang that couldn't shoot straight," the bumbling pair somehow managed to get their anchor line entangled with his and nearly swamped both boats.

Cold and wet, with a boat that wouldn't run and a very angry Mexican captain shouting at them, they again decided they'd had enough. So they loaded the boat back on its trailer and stopped by our house to say good-bye before once again heading home to Michigan.

This time we were *sure* we'd seen the last of these men and their gospel cabin cruiser—that they were *finally* ready to consider that, just possibly, God may not have given them the boat to evangelize lost Indians after all.

But I should have known they wouldn't give up so easily.

A couple of years later I met one of the cabin cruiser men in a church in Mexico City. Proudly and excitedly he told me he was living on an island in the Gulf of Mexico, only a few hundred yards off the Mexican Coast. He was happy as a clam to be using his gospel boat to do his shopping and pick up his mail on the mainland.

LORD, SOMETIMES I'VE ALSO TRIED TO GET YOUR STAMP OF APPROVAL ON MY OWN PLANS AND DESIRES. HELP ME TO LISTEN TO YOUR VOICE. AND TO THE COUNSEL OF OTHERS. EVEN WHEN IT ISN'T WHAT I WANT TO HEAR.

To those who use well what they are given, even more will be given, and they will have an abundance. But for those who are unfaithful, even what little they have will be taken away.
Matthew 25:29

PROPHET UNAWARE

"What if I told you we will take away our airplane in three years?" I blurted.

The faces of the missionaries registered pure shock. "You can't do that," said one. "We can't survive here without the plane," another shouted. "Why would you do that?" said another. Everyone in the group was suddenly united against me.

All, that is, except one woman. "Make it four years and I'll be finished," she said quietly.

I had threatened impulsively to remove our airplane, out of sheer exasperation with the missionaries. I had no idea that I was being prophetic.

We were deep in the Amazon jungles of southern Guyana, near the Brazilian border. This was ten years before the mass suicide of the followers of cult leader Jim Jones put "Jonestown" and the little country of Guyana on front pages around the world. I had gone there to evaluate our air service to missionaries who worked with jungle Indians. There were absolutely no roads into that region. The missionaries depended on our airplane for their very survival.

As I tried to learn more about their plans and future needs, it became increasingly apparent that these people had no clear goals. They seemed to feel they were heroic missionaries just because they were living in an exotic place. I'd met a few other individual missionaries like that in my travels, but never a whole group in one place. That's why I impulsively decided to shock them, just to get their attention.

The one exception in the group was a woman who was translating the New Testament into a local language. Her goal was very clear. Four more years and she would be finished.

Perhaps God was as exasperated with those missionaries as I was. At any rate he didn't wait three years. Instead, a mere *three weeks* after my visit everything they had was suddenly taken away from them. Our airplane was impounded by the government and all missionaries in the interior were expelled. All, that is, except one.

Here's how it happened: About 130 years ago, right after the American Civil War, a few former Confederate soldiers who couldn't stand to live under Yankee rule moved to southern Guyana. There, in a natural grassland in the heart of the jungle, they set up cattle ranches and trained local Indians as cowboys. Somehow their descendants managed to maintain U.S. citizenship through several subsequent generations. A few days after my visit to southern Guyana, those "American" ranchers armed their cowboys, blocked all the airstrips in the area, and declared their region independent. They planned to detach their region from Guyana and join it to Venezuela. Our mission pilot tipped off the Guyana government by radio and the government quickly squelched the uprising. (The government impounded our airplane anyway, but it was eventually released.)

Since the leaders of the rebellion were, technically, American citizens, the government decided to expel *all* Americans from southern Guyana. All, that is, except one American woman—the Bible translator—who had a clear goal. There was no logical reason why the government should have made that one exception.

It's not hard to find fault with those missionaries who were resting on their laurels, without clear goals or purpose. But how easy it is for me to fall into the same trap . . . to find myself thinking I must be special just because I am in "full-time service" for God.

By contrast, that woman translator was special because she had her priorities in order.

LORD, KEEP ME FROM LAZINESS AND SPIRITUAL PRIDE . . . FROM COASTING ALONG ON SPIRITUAL DECISIONS I MADE LONG AGO.

God saved you by his special favor when you believed.
And you can't take credit for this; it is a gift of God.
Ephesians 2:8

PLAYING INDIANA JONES

When I circled low over the strange clump of trees, I found myself looking down the steps of a tall Mayan pyramid.

When I was a kid we played Tarzan. These days boys are more likely to play Indiana Jones, pretending to slash through the jungle and stumble across the ruins of an ancient lost city. Not many boys get to live out those fantasies, but I did. In fact, I actually discovered the ruins of two different lost cities in the jungles of Yucatan and Chiapas.

The central Yucatan jungle is as flat as a carpet—no clearings, no rivers, not even a stream. Before the tourist mecca of Cancún was built in the 1960s there were no roads of any kind through that jungle. As I flew across it one day, thick clouds forced me lower and lower until I was flying just above the treetops. That's when I saw it. Up ahead a clump of taller trees stood out above all the rest. "That's strange," I thought. "There are no hills in this area."

As I circled low and peered down through the tall trees, I saw they were growing on the sides of a Mayan pyramid—a big one, completely unknown to archaeologists. What's more, its style was from the Classic Period, at least 400 years older than Chichen Itza and the other well-known Mayan ruins of Yucatan. As we found out later, the pyramid I had spotted was only one of several that formed two ceremonial centers, joined by a mile-long stone causeway, much like a Roman road.

The other ancient ruin I discovered was at least a thousand years older. Shortly after sunrise on a crystal clear day I flew alone across an uninhabited stretch of the Lacandon jungle near the Guatemala border. Since there were no people in that area back then, Mexican pilots rarely flew there. As I crossed a low mountain range, I noticed a stone pinnacle on top, like a big inverted cone or rounded pyramid. The low angle of the early morning sunlight was just right, and for a brief instant I caught a glimpse of a wall of cut stones near the top of the pinnacle.

"That looks like an Olmecan ruin," I thought. So I dived down and flew around the pinnacle with my wingtip only a few yards away. Sure enough, all around the top of the inverted cone I saw walls of stone, cut in classic Olmecan style. On top of the pinnacle was a flat space just big enough for a wooden temple that had long since rotted away.

The Olmecs had built their temple on the tip of a natural pyramid in a setting that was far higher and more awesome than any of the later Mayan pyramids.

The Olmecan culture predated the Mayas by at least a thousand years. In fact, it flourished around the time of King David and King Solomon and had already disappeared before the time of Christ. All that remains of that entire civilization are 17 massive, helmeted stone heads weighing up to 20 tons each, plus a few scattered walls and stone carvings and some small human figures carved in jade. Nothing else is left from a culture that covered a fifth of modern Mexico.

Before my two discoveries, archaeologists had already spent entire lifetimes studying the many Mayan and Olmecan ruins in southeast Mexico and Guatemala, but neither of the ruins I found was on their maps. (I reported them and they are now.)

Around the time King Solomon's stonecutters were building the first great Jewish temple, Olmecan stonecutters—working without metal tools—were also shaping massive stones to terrace that mountaintop pinnacle. How did they manage to lift those stones so high? What drove them to such amazing efforts? What gods were they trying to please?

Did they ever imagine that all their hard work would someday return to jungle and be forgotten?

As I flew on that morning, I pondered—as I have many times since—what I did to merit being born in a time and place where I would have the opportunity to hear about Christ. Sometimes I tend to act like it was my own clever idea to be born in the twentieth century and in a Christian home. But, of course, neither you nor I have anything to do with choosing our parents—or when or where we are born.

Why were my parents not worshippers of the gods of the Mayas or Olmecs. Or followers of Hindu gods or the Allah of Islam? Those were the questions running through my head as I flew on across the jungle that morning. Oh, I know the theological answer, "God's grace." But that doesn't entirely explain it nor satisfy.

Maybe "God's love" comes closer.

LORD, I DON'T MERIT YOUR LOVE ANY MORE THAN THE ANCIENT MAYAS AND OLMECS DID. HELP ME TO SPEND MY LIFE ON THINGS THAT REALLY MATTER.

> *Whoever clings to this life will lose it,*
> *and whoever loses this life will save it.*
> Luke 17:33

ROOM IN A FIVE-STAR MONASTERY

A sagging cot in a decaying stone building on a mountain-top. That's what I pictured when I heard we would be meeting in a monastery in Lebanon. I even wondered whether there would be a bathroom. To my utter amazement, the monastery turned out to be an ultramodern building with solid marble floors and mosaic tile walls.

I had gone to Beirut in the spring of 1996 for a conference of Arab pastors and church leaders from all over the Middle East. The long brutal civil war in Lebanon had only recently ended, so I expected to find a city in ruins. Instead, I saw hundreds of shiny new apartment buildings covering the mountain sides. Half the cars seemed to be Mercedes and upscale clothing stores competed for space with new Pizza Hut and KFC restaurants.

My room in the monastery was as fancy as any five-star hotel. I walked out on my own private balcony and found myself looking down on the glistening coast of the Mediterranean 2,000 feet below. Wow! And that was only the first of many surprises I experienced in Lebanon, the most paradoxical of all the countries I've ever visited.

A group of Egyptian Christians invited me to go with them to the ski slopes about an hour outside Beirut. As we drove through the mountains I saw huge Catholic churches towering over every village—but not a Muslim mosque in sight. In the ski area, hundreds of people dressed in the latest ski fashions zoomed down the snowy slopes. Scores of European style chalets were perched on the hillsides. All the advertising signs were in French, not Arabic. I felt like I'd suddenly been transported back to Switzerland, where I used to live. "How could this possibly be the Muslim Middle East?" I puzzled.

It's easy to conclude from our news media that all the people in the Middle East are sinister Arabs or Iranian terrorists, ready to bomb or shoot anyone who opposes them. Not true. Millions of Christians have coexisted with Muslims in the Arab World ever since the seventh century. In fact, about *15 million* people in the Arab world today consider themselves to be Christians, not Muslims.

Most of these Christians in the Middle East belong to historic churches that date back to the second or third centuries . . . Egyptian Copts, Syrian Orthodox, Chaldeans, Armenians, Maronites, Greek Orthodox, and several others, each at least as different from the rest in doctrine and liturgy as Catholics differ from Protestants. Of course some of these people are Christians only by tradition. Over the centuries they have been marginalized and oppressed by the Muslim majority and have managed to survive only by carefully avoiding any semblance of "proselytizing" Muslims.

Many other Christians in the 18 countries of the Arab World are evangelicals. In some countries they number only a dozen or two, in others many thousands. Until recently, these evangelicals were divided along the denominational lines of the former European missionaries, but Arab believers have begun to ignore their denominational differences and form coalitions. I went to Beirut at the invitation of the largest of those interdenominational coalitions.

During my stay in that "five-star monastery" in Lebanon I was absolutely amazed by the vision and spiritual maturity of the Arab evangelical leaders. They had come from all over the Arab World—even from Iraq and Kuwait—in order to worship, pray, plan together, and share their victories and defeats with each other.

Our Western media bombards us with stories about fanatical Muslim suicide bombers and terrorists. In Lebanon I met equally courageous Arab *Christians* who represent the Prince of Peace. *They* are the real hope for the Arab World.

I was astounded, during my visit to Lebanon, by the economic boom and lack of visible effects from the war. I left there feeling that perhaps peace had finally come to that troubled land. But once gain I was fooled by outward appearances.

Barely one week after I left Lebanon the Israeli army again attacked that troubled little country, shelling the suburbs of Beirut and killing hundreds of people who had huddled in a U.N. refugee camp in the south. An American friend who lives in Beirut kept sending us urgent e-mail messages, pleading for our help and describing the helicopter gunships that were hovering offshore and blasting away at the houses all around him. Such is life in that land of paradox and enigma called Lebanon.

Sometimes it seems God takes delight in paradox. Jesus often used it to grab the attention of his listeners. What could be more paradoxical than saying you will lose your life if you cling to it and save your life if you give it up? Seemingly contradictory, nevertheless true.

Just as I found Lebanon to be totally different from what I had pictured, so also does God refuse to conform to my stereotypes of him. But, then, if we could predict him, he wouldn't be God, would he?

LORD, THANK YOU FOR YOUR COURAGEOUS SERVANTS IN THE ARAB WORLD. AND PLEASE HELP ME NOT TO STEREOTYPE OTHER PEOPLE . . . OR YOU.

And everyone who has given up houses or brothers or sisters or
father or mother or children or property, for my sake, will receive a
hundred times as much in return and will have eternal life.
Matthew 19:29

OUR FATHERS KNEW BEST

"**W**e didn't have to discuss it. When he told us he wanted to rent a piece of our tribal land to a *kashlán* Mexican outsider, we looked at each other and knew he must die."

That's the way Juan Pérez Jolote, one of the elders of the Chamula tribe, described why they had killed another of their tribal elders— merely for suggesting that an outsider be allowed to farm a piece of their land.

For 100,000 Chamula Mayas of Chiapas, change is the ultimate evil. They live right on the outskirts of the Mexican city of San Cristobal de Las Casas, yet they have somehow managed to preserve their tribal religion and the customs of their ancestors over the nearly 500 years since the Spaniards first arrived there.

The Chamula ceremonial center is an old colonial Catholic church, but there is nothing Catholic about their religion. On the dirt floor of that church they burn candles at the spots where their traditions tell them their ancient Mayan gods were buried. Their real god is the sun, and the moon they call Mary. They killed the last Catholic priest who tried to live among them. That was over 150 years ago.

In our Western culture we have enshrined *change* as good—in fact, almost as our god. We clamor to buy products that are *newer, bigger, better, or faster.* We choose leaders who promise us the most change. We assume that anyone who sees a "better" product will want it. It's hard for us to imagine that half the people on earth see change as bad. For them, the ideal leader is the person who most successfully *resists* change.

Among the Chamulas, change is incredibly risky. The spirits of the dead are always among them, as real to them as their own bodies. And those spirits—even the spirits of their own parents and grandparents— are extremely unpredictable and vindictive. "If anything at all changes," they reason, "even the footpath beside your house, the spirits might get angry and cause sickness or death. Better not to risk it. Better to dress the same, farm the same, and worship exactly the same as our ancestors. If we build a new house, we must make sure to use some materials from an old one."

"Our fathers knew best about everything!" they firmly believe.

Not all traditional cultures live in as much terror of vindictive spirits as the Chamulas do, but almost all traditional cultures believe their fathers' ways were better.

When my friend Benton Rhodes was assigned to direct a mission farm in the mountains of Ecuador, he decided to experiment with hybrid corn. The results were fantastic, four or five times as much as the local variety. One day he was out in the cornfield admiring his handiwork when he heard two Indians talking as they approached. They hadn't spotted him, so he squatted down to listen, expecting to hear them admiring his spectacular crop. Instead he heard them laughing and ridiculing the stupid foreigner who planted his corn stalks "this far apart" when everyone knows you should plant them "this far apart."

Increased production was irrelevant. The important thing was to plant corn the way their fathers had always done.

Eavesdropping on that conversation changed the direction of Benton's life. He went on to lead an organization that specializes in *appropriate* innovations in agriculture among poor people around the world.

Walking across the city square of Campeche one evening, I bumped into a man whom I had met before, in a church in a small village 200 miles away. He told me he had traveled all the way to Campeche in order to claim a large plot of free homestead land from the government— enough land so each of his sons would inherit a good farm.

This man was far more entrepreneurial than most in his village. He was young, strong, energetic and resourceful enough to fight through all the red tape to claim new land. As we chatted, I asked him if he had ever heard of hybrid corn. "Sure," he replied. "In fact, the government will give us free hybrid seeds in exchange for our native seeds."

"Do you know anyone who has planted it?" I asked.

"Yes, one of my neighbors planted some." "How did it do?"

"Oh, fine! It had two or three big ears on each stalk." (Theirs usually has only one.)

"Have you ever thought of planting hybrid corn yourself?" His face registered a look of pure puzzlement that I'll never forget as he reflected on my question for several seconds.

Finally he softly replied, "No, I have never considered it." Corn, or *maíz*, was first domesticated in the very area where this man lived. In fact the elaborate religion of his Mayan ancestors was centered around studying the heavens to determine the precise dates when they should burn their fields to prepare for planting and precisely when they should plant their corn in order to take advantage of the rains.

My friend planted his corn exactly like his ancestors had done for thousands of years. Why should he risk using some different method proposed by bureaucrats in the Ministry of Agriculture? He *knew* the methods of his fathers would work. As for the government methods, "*¿Quién sabe?* Who knows?"

Traditional societies do change, of course. When the first few Chamulas became Christians, my wife and I lived only three miles from their tribal center—the same place where, a few years earlier, they had killed the tribal elder for merely suggesting they should rent a piece of land to an outsider.

A few weeks after the first group of Chamulas became Christians, their neighbors attacked them and soon drove them into exile. More than once the new believers had to lie flat on the floor while neighbors fired bullets through the flimsy walls of their huts.

Once a group of Chamula men surrounded a house where the Christians were meeting. The attackers had fortified themselves with liquor for courage and were determined to kill all the "traitors" to their traditions. Suddenly other men in shining white appeared between them and the house. The attackers fled in terror. Later one of the attackers met Miguel, leader of the Chamula Christians, in the nearby Mexican market town of San Cristobal. He told Miguel about the men in shining white who had frightened them away, then asked, "What kind of devils do you Christians have, anyway?"

Four children of Chamula Christians were sleeping alone when they heard a noise outside. When the oldest opened the door, she took a shotgun blast in the stomach. Two men then ran in, slashing at the children with machetes and setting fire to the house. Miraculously, only one child died. Later one of the children—an eight year old girl—stood bravely before her attackers in a police lineup in San Cristobal and boldly challenged, "Have you no shame?"

We hired some of the Chamula Christian exiles to do odd jobs until they could find more permanent work. So we came to know their courage and commitment extremely well.

All that was nearly 30 years ago. Ever since then a steady stream of Chamulas have been coming to Christ, even though they know the cost. The tribal elders still guard the status quo. Every new believer is still driven into exile, losing house and land. *Thirty thousand* believers are in exile thus far.

A few years ago my friend, Miguel, leader of the first small group of Chamula believers—a man who had escaped death over and over again—was finally killed by the tribal elders. And still the new believers come.

LORD, I WASN'T AN OUTCAST WHEN I LEFT HOME AND RELATIVES TO BE A MISSIONARY. HOW WOULD I REACT IF I FACED THE ALL-OR-NOTHING CHOICES THE CHAMULA BELIEVERS AND MILLIONS OF OTHERS LIKE THEM FACE TODAY? GIVE ME COURAGE TO CONFESS YOU, WHATEVER THE COST.

*The Spirit of the Lord is upon me, for he has appointed me to preach
Good News to the poor. He has sent me to proclaim that captives will be
released, that the blind will see, that the downtrodden will be
freed from their oppressors.*

Luke 4:18

TILL THEY HAVE FACES

Deep in the jungles of Ecuador I once met a man who
literally had no face.

The man was a Shuar Indian, in rags. The Shuar, better known as
Jivaros, are the people who invented head shrinking long before psychia-
trists thought of the idea. A tropical disease had eaten away the man's
nose, eyelids and lips. Scar tissue had grown smoothly across the eyes.
There was a hole where his nose should have been and there were teeth
and gums, but otherwise no semblance of a face. Just flat skin.

I still remember the flood of emotions I felt as I stared at him . . .
shock, sympathy, revulsion, curiosity.

But as I gazed on this man with no face, I immediately thought about
how he symbolizes the masses of people in our world—billions of people
who have dreams, hopes, fears and frustrations just like we do, but who
are forced to live out their lives in poverty, desperation and powerless-
ness, then pass from the scene and never leave a mark. *People without
faces,* in terms of the power and status values of our world.

In a somewhat different sense, whatever our education or fame or
power, we are all "faceless" until we find our true personality in Christ.
C.S. Lewis wrote an allegory entitled *Till We Have Faces* in which he
attempted to show that we can only discover our true identity when we
give control of our lives to God. However, at least three billion people in
our world today—mostly poor people—have no idea that they are of
infinite value to God . . . that, in the midst of their frustration and despair,
he is anxious to give them true faces . . . inner meaning . . . worth.

The irony is that God is working today through thousands of indigenous missionaries who are "faceless" in a different way—in the sense
that they are unknown and will never be honored by the outside world.
These unsung heroes of the faith are bringing hope and salvation to the
faceless billions around the world who do not know God.

These Christian brothers and sisters are sacrificing material success and risking their families, their health, their safety and even their personal freedom in order to give compassionate help to their faceless countrymen . . . to tell them that God already knows and loves them . . . that they have their identity in him . . . that he wants to give them true faces.

We all know that God does not look on our appearance or status or fame, but on our hearts. We know this in our heads, but how easily and often do we forget it in our daily walk.

*   *   *   *   *

When I met the faceless man in the jungles of Ecuador, he had only recently become a Christian. He smiled as he told me, through an interpreter, how happy he was and how well he was being treated by other Christians. I can't explain how I could tell that a man with no face was smiling. But I *knew* he was smiling. I think he was smiling because he understood that some day God is going to give him a *real* face.

LORD, GIVE ME THE SIMPLE FAITH OF YOUR SERVANTS ON THE FRONTIERS OF FAITH. AND LET ME NEVER COOL IN MY PASSION TO SHARE YOUR LOVE BY WORD AND DEED WITH THE FACELESS MILLIONS WHO HAVE YET TO FIND THEIR TRUE IDENTITY IN YOU.

About Partners International

   With more than 50 years experience, Partners International is a recognized leader in partnering with indigenous Christian ministries in the non-Western world, linking resources from Christians in the West with Third-World agencies that minister to both physically and spiritually needy people.

   The Partners team emphasizes local self-sufficiency and avoids creating unhealthy dependency. It works only with indigenous ministries that have proven track records. Its priorities are evangelism, grassroots leadership training, economic self-help and church planting.

   Partners International currently provides financial support for 3,300 indigenous Christian workers in over 40 of the world's least evangelized countries, often in places where Western missionaries are not allowed. Every year these workers win about 40,000 new believers to Christ. They also provide many humanitarian services, train some 30,000 local Christian leaders each year, and start an average of one new church in an unchurched community every 15 hours.

2302 Zanker Road, Suite 100, P.O. Box 15025,
San Jose, California 95115-0025
(800) 966-5515, www.partnersintl.org